Kevin Nichols

REFRACTING THE LIGHT
Learning the Languages of Faith

First published 1997 by
Lindisfarne Books
7-8 Lower Abbey Street
Dublin 1

Available in the UK from:
Veritas Book & Video Distribution Ltd
Lower Avenue
Leamington Spa
Warwickshire CV31 3NP

Lindisfarne is an imprint of Veritas Publications

ISBN 1 85390 343 4

British Library Cataloguing
in Publication Data.
A catalogue record for
this book is available
from the British Library.

The author and publishers are grateful to Faber & Faber Ltd and
Doubleday & Co. Inc. for permission to reproduce extracts from
Collected Poems 1909-1962 by T. S. Eliot; and to Faber & Faber
Ltd for extracts from The Idea of Order at Key West' by Wallace
Stevens.

Cover design by Bill Bolger
Cover illustration by Science Photo Library
Printed in the Republic of Ireland by Betaprint Ltd, Dublin

REFRACTING THE LIGHT

CONTENTS

Foreword ✠ David Konstant, Bishop of Leeds   7

Preface   9

Introduction
Faith: Language and Reality   11

1   The Truth of Imagination
    The Language of Story   23

2   'A Blessed Rage for Order'
    The Language of Doctrine   51

3   Feeling and Form
    The Language of Liturgy   72

4   The Truth in Love
    The Language of Morality   96

5 At Chartres
   A Meditation on the Simple and the Complex   130

Notes   153

Select Bibliography   156

FOREWORD

Mystery beckons us to reach inside itself, to fathom it, know it, grasp it and so to make it our own. In order to express our experience of mystery we use words. These words may unlock, unravel, unwrap our experience, so that through reflection and contemplation truth is illumined. And yet these same words may also in some measure confuse and puzzle so that the mystery is even further confounded. We rapidly discover this twin effect of the use of words – that they have the power both to release the inner meaning of mystery, and at the same time, because of the limitations of language, to constrict its meaning.

The words of this book are wonderfully chosen. Ideas and words tumble about and nudge each other into position so that the reader begins to reach almost unconsciously into the depth of mystery. There are 'implicit questions which are in all our hearts … which engage the imagination and the heart'. We explore the languages of story, doctrine, liturgy and morality; we are drawn into the drama of our own growth as we recognise more clearly the richness of our everyday experience; we are weaned away from any tendency to a narrow fundamentalism as the sweep of the mystery of our faith is shown us.

Kevin Nichols is poet, theologian, story teller, artist, teacher and believer. He offers a rich fare to those who want to grow in faith. He understands the strength and weakness of language, relishes image and metaphor, knows that the simple and complex must stand together, teases out meaning and importance from the ordinary realities of the world. In all this he accompanies us in our search for truth, and does so with a touch that delights.

I warmly commend this lovely book to all pilgrims for truth. St Augustine advises: 'Let us seek so as to find, and having found let us continue our search'. Here is a fine tool for our continuing search.

✠ David Konstant
Bishop of Leeds

PREFACE

This book grew out of a course taught over several years in the Diocese of Hexham and Newcastle; and it is in the area of Adult Christian Education that I hope it may be of more general use. Its focus is the dilemma between the experience of faith and its several formulations. I have called these the languages of faith and have chosen four; the narrative expression of faith, doctrinal formulas, the liturgy and Christian morality. Perhaps this is a rather arbitrary choice but I am encouraged to see that the structure chosen by the Catechism of the Catholic Church – faith professed, celebrated, lived – embodies a similar approach.

I have not taken the word 'learning' these languages to mean acquiring a large amount of content material. Rather I have seen it as gaining a familiarity with these languages and a degree of fluency in them; as, to extend the metaphor, learning their grammar and syntax.

I warmly thank those friends and colleagues who have shared in teaching the course or who have read the manuscript and made helpful suggestions: especially Cynthia Conway, Margaret Dodds, Elizabeth Hughes, Peter Phillips and Adrian Towers. I thank Isabel Emmett and Anne Dillon who have typed and processed the text; and my editor Fiona Biggs whose editorial motto is, quite rightly, 'suaviter in modo, fortiter in re'. I am glad to dedicate this little book to all my teachers and all my students, with love.

Kevin Nichols
25 August 1997

INTRODUCTION

Faith: Language and Reality

New towns sprout around its shores and raw settlements eat away at the desert. Yet the Sea of Galilee does not disappoint. It is the jewel of Israel. England is sea-girt, the oceans its defensive moat. Galilee has the desert for a moat and the sea is its heart. The farms cluster close, sharp, geometric belts of green: lemon, orange, grapefruit, pineapple, banana. They suck life from the lake but the lake has plenty of life to give. Across from Tiberias the Golan Heights loom dark and sinister. Only yesterday, it seems, these ridges were crowned with Syrian guns, their long barrels sweeping and ranging over village and crossroad, over city, kibbutz and market. I lift up my eyes to the mountains, from whence shall come my help? It is a cockpit of life; building and destruction, fruitfulness and threat, conflict and harmony, enlightenment and bigotry jostle together. It is a proscenium arch that encloses the drama of our destiny.

Squalls come suddenly. They seem to blow in from nowhere, from a serene sky. The skin of the water darkens, wrinkles, then erupts. Mist, spume, confusion. In the aftermath, sitting on a rock under a clearing sky, the water settling to a gentle chop, it is easy to imagine that the winds of time could also blow clear; easy to visualise a pair of talkative fishermen knotting their broken nets on the beach. Perhaps the call of Jesus, 'Come follow me', did not seem particularly momentous; something to do and see, a break in the dreary routine. Perhaps there was some deeper compulsion. We admire the promptitude of their response and would like to think it the archetype of our own.

> In simple trust like theirs who heard
> Beside the Syrian sea
> The gracious calling of the Lord
> Let us, like them, without a word
> Rise up and follow Thee.

It was to be a journey during which they would often be disconcerted and sometimes pushed to the limit; moaning and cursing as they negotiated the goats' paths in the hills round Jericho, chilled to the bone on the road to Jerusalem in midwinter:

> A cold coming we had of it,
> Just the worst time of year
> For a journey, and such a long journey.[1]

Their travels through the terrain of the mind and the heart and the imagination were still more unsettling. Such things they heard; such strange, unaccountable, alarming, disorienting, marvellous things. 'Blessed are the poor... theirs is the kingdom.'[2] How could this be? 'Before Abraham was I am.'[3] What could this mean? How far it was from the down-to-earth speech of their Galilean neighbours. How often they came to long for that blunt plainness which calls a spade a spade. 'If you are the Son of God tell us plainly.'[4] 'Master, we do not know where you are going, how can we know the way?'[5] They got plenty of vivid stories but not too many plain answers. Instead they learned that God is indeed a new language. Eventually, after many false starts, some failures and a few tragedies, they came to speak that language pretty well.

Language, faith and revelation

Learning a foreign language at school used to be a chore which brought few rewards. The learner might amass a substantial vocabulary, might successfully master irregular verbs and plurals. She might be able to speak well about things she did not particularly want to say; but she would find a conversation about something complex or something personal, barely comprehensible, halting and unsatisfactory. To achieve fluency, to click into the rhythm of phrases and idioms, to be able to reach for words and constructions with relative ease, this was a moment of liberation. Quite suddenly perhaps, strange territory became familiar and real communication possible. For adults this fluency does not come out of the blue. A grasp of gender, of auxiliary verbs, of the function of pronouns is its pre-condition, forms its scaffolding. But it cannot guarantee the achievement of fluency. There is language as a network of rules and structures. There is language as an element in which we live and relate; as we hope faith might be, like the air we breathe, like the home we inhabit.

Faith, indeed, seeks understanding. It seeks to learn new languages. This is not for the sake of intellectual curiosity nor to transform faith into a rational ideology. Rather it is because understanding breeds confidence, opens vision, makes possible communication and makes plain the implications and the requirements of faith. In language, a grasp of how the pluperfect works enables us to catch the sense of timing and succession. In faith, to grasp a doctrine or respond to a symbol enables us to understand our experience of the world differently, to think more expansively, to see how we should act. There is faith as a response, as a 'blik', as a vision. There is faith as a coherent system of beliefs, as ritual celebration, as a way of life and a code of morality.

We use the word 'faith', sometimes in the one sense, sometimes in the other. The statement 'He has deep faith' points to a personal gift, a virtue, a relationship. To speak of 'teaching *the* faith' implies something which can be expressed and communicated systematically. Both of these views of faith are valid. It is a response, it is a gift, it is the first of the theological virtues. On the other hand it is also a heritage of understanding which is to be cherished with care, to be preached and taught with fidelity. Its end is not a proposition but a person. Yet personal response contains and implies knowledge which can be understood and formulated.

In the liturgy we are required to 'proclaim the *mysteries* of faith'. We acknowledge that its object is a mysterious reality, not a pedestrian fact. Yet 'mystery' is a word which has fallen on hard times. One of the failings of the modern mind is to be constantly transforming mysteries into problems. For problem-solving is popular; problems are the meat and drink of a technological age. So the word 'mystery' survives mainly in phrases like 'murder mystery' and 'mystery tour'. It is a puzzle, an enigma, but the answer will become totally clear on the last page or at the last stop. The older meaning of mystery, the one found in the liturgy, is a different one. It connotes a truth which is of such range and depth as to be beyond total comprehension by the human mind. This does not mean that it is meaningless, like a contradiction or a surd. It is not completely inaccessible to the mind. We can express facets of it, formulate truths about it, even say clearly what is does *not* mean. But its total meaning eludes us. Moreover, unlike more limited kinds of truth, it does not yield its meaning only to systematic and objective logic. Feeling, sensibility and wisdom in the biblical sense can lead us towards it. For there is a logic of the heart as well as a logic of the head. Poetry, it has been said, is language pushed to the furthermost possibilities of meaning.

These considerations help us to understand why St Paul speaks of faith as seeing 'through a glass darkly'. It is a form of seeing, as understanding is, as when we say, 'I see the point'. But this understanding (the 'language') is subordinate to the 'obedience of faith' of which St Paul also speaks. Faith is first a personal response to God and secondly an assent to his truths. To say that is to see that there is a parallel duality in our understanding of God's revelation to us.

The word 'revelation' also has its ambiguities. The headline 'Sensational Revelations' implies the unwelcome discovery of hidden facts. The phrase 'a revealing remark', however, usually means that what is disclosed is not so much fact or meaning as motive or attitude. The speaker reveals what he is like; or reveals something he is unable or unwilling to say openly. He reveals a 'hidden agenda' which lies deeper and is more worthy of note than his explicit remarks.

In our understanding of God's revelation to us there is, it is often said, a deep divide between the idea of God revealing himself and the idea of God revealing truths about himself. There is something in this. Probably most accounts of revelation veer in the one direction or the other. Yet the distinction is not black and white. The idea of a self-revelation absolutely without content is hardly comprehensible. Love at first sight may sometimes happen. Equally some people may be given a mystical experience of God which is not mediated by knowledge. But for the most part, love involves knowledge and grows with it. We reveal ourselves to those we trust and trust is the beginning of love. God's gift of himself is not without content. It includes some knowledge of him.

On the other hand, an account of revelation which focuses on truths about God can scarcely justify its name. It is as though God came into the world and then went away, leaving his luggage behind him. I may learn facts about a person by reading a form. But unless the facts inhere in some way in a relationship, in the gift of self, the word revelation can hardly be justified.

Von Hugel's dilemma[6]

In religion there is the experience and there are the formulations. Von Hugel's dilemma was (and is) this: experience always has vitality and energy but it is difficult to communicate; formulations are easy to communicate but they readily go dead. Most of our difficulties in religious education (evangelisation too) pivot round this dilemma. Let us explore its terms a little.

'Experience', whichever way we look at it, is an elusive, protean word. It is often opposed to theory, often supposed to be a source of wisdom (*experientia docet* – or as Mr Micawber put it, '*experientia* does it'), sometimes taken as an acid-test of truth (does it ring true to your experience?). With a complex word like this it is not useful to attempt the sort of neat definition which dictionaries offer. But we can try, more roughly, to map the geography of its meaning.

In referring to our own experience we are likely to say 'I feel' rather than 'I believe' or 'I know'. This suggests that experience is more closely allied to the world of emotion than to the world of knowledge or conviction. Yet experience is not *an* emotion to be listed along with the feelings of anger and grief. We use the word in a different register. Even if we added up the sum of all our emotions we should have to say that experience contains other elements as well, and goes beyond them. All the same there is a kinship between experience and feeling; and this is to be found in the character of immediacy or directness which both have. What is thought or known is by that very fact distanced and held at arm's length. Feeling or experiencing brings us into direct contact with a reality, a state of affairs or a person; and this immediacy generates vividness and vitality in the act.

In addition to its ambiguous relationship with feeling, the word 'experience' is often connected with the idea of process and this connection is also an enlightening one. Having a concept, holding a belief or reaching a logical conclusion are acts which exist in a realm of meaning dominated by fixity, by permanence. Experience on the other hand exists in a horizon of fluidity. Its contents change, its contours alter, it may expand or contract, its inner order may fragment and re-unify in a different pattern. The changeableness of experience, far from being a symptom of weakness, indicates its strength, its capacity to deepen and expand. 'Here below, to live is to change and to be perfect is to have changed often.' It is easy to see how experience contains an engaging energy which formulations lack; also why it cannot be packaged in ways convenient for learning.

An account of the idea of experience given by Henry James expresses vividly both its elusiveness and its immediacy.

> [Experience is] an immense sensibility, a kind of huge spider-web of the finest silken threads suspended in the chamber of consciousness and catching every airborne particle in its tissue. It is the very atmosphere of the mind.

What then of the experience of faith? Firstly, its directness is not that of mystical experience, in which there occurs direct, immediate contact with the transcendent godhead. The history of spirituality shows that this mystical vision occurs rarely and only in special circumstances: and is a radical transformation of human experience. The experience of faith is more common and more earthbound than that.

Secondly, experience is never 'content-free'. It makes no sense to try to think of 'sheer experience', detached from ideas, attitudes and symbols. Those who have the experience of faith either emerge from or are in contact with a community and a tradition; the experience is nourished and given body by the stories, concepts and symbols which constitute that tradition. What distinguishes the experience from a bundle of formulas is the way in which it is held together. It is a dimension of personal life; that unique and intricate network of hopes and dilemmas, of fears and affections, of need for affirmation and meaning. That is the 'huge spider-web' which catches the components in its tissue. The experience of faith is not blind. It has its reasons but they are the reasons of the heart.

Set against the immediacy of experience is the distance of form or structure. We speak of 'society' or of 'the establishment' and are able to hold these things at arm's length. That they are not part of our immediate experience does not mean that they cannot be analysed and debated with passion. That they can be thus held, 'pinned and wriggling to the wall', is what constitutes them as formulations. They fall into the arena of our common scrutiny, are open to public debate, public analysis, public tests for truth.

As well as structures, which are the business of the sociologist, these are also logical formulations which are the frequent concern of philosophers and theologians; sets of concepts logically jointed and organised. Let us take as an example the Catholic doctrine of the Church. This contains historical argument (What do the gospels foreshadow?) and legal theory (What is the nature of the Church's authority? What is its proper structure?). The recent and helpful discussions of 'models of the Church' weigh the validity and value of these diverse logical strands.

In an intricate and subtle area of life such as faith, it is not likely that the common formulations which emerge will be logically homogeneous or neat. However, the idea of structures, forms and formulations is not restricted to the world of clinical logic, empirical investigation or social enquiry. The idea of 'form' is also crucial in the arts.

An artist creates sensible forms which express human feeling. These forms are not, as we sometimes mistakenly imply, spontaneous and undisciplined, a 'fine careless rapture'. They – the sounds and images of a poem, the shapes and colours of a painting – require at every point a disciplined sensibility, a high intelligence, a 'blessed rage for order'. To work they require to be as tightly organised as a vigorous logical analysis. Among the expressions of faith – its languages – some have a close kinship with the arts; notably the stories and poetry of Scripture, the mosaic of symbol, movement, sound and silence which form the liturgy. There is sensibility as well as sense, there is a logic of the heart as well as a logic of the brain. Forms of all kinds do not derive their unity and force from being part of our personal 'spider-web'. What compels us is that the forms themselves are logically or imaginatively convincing.

Languages of faith

The vivid faith-experience of the early followers of Christ had to find a voice and find it quickly. Christians spoke to each other, not only as an overflowing of their full hearts but also to enrich one another's experience; to teach and to learn. Moreover, they were left with a missionary commission, *'Go, teach all the nations'.* How would they preach and teach the faith to those brought up on the rich heritage of the law and the prophets? How would they present it in the Greek world, more sceptical, more analytical, more abstract? These were not questions which were coldly addressed. But they were concerns, more obscurely active and anxious.

The earliest way of speaking the faith was, it seems, an account of the life and words of Jesus, handed on by word of mouth, and finding, over a few years, a fixed form. This body of teaching, this catechesis, was used by the writers of the gospels. Although it stood close to the initial faith-experience of the disciples of Jesus it was, to an extent, formalised; organised in view of the understanding of the writer and the needs of his hearers. Stories and sayings were ordered so that the main lines of force in the Lord's teaching might appear.

Out of this simple teaching there soon emerged a 'salvation-history'; in effect, another way of speaking faith. St Paul, having arrived in Athens and taken the temperature of the city, radically adjusted his style of preaching. Facing an audience of philosophers he spoke of the unity of the human race and its varied search for truth under God's providence. He struck a new note, trying to reconcile faith and reason. It was not a successful venture but the challenge was picked up later by the apologists who made use of philosophical ideas and logical arguments and wrote that all human learning contains traces of God's truth, for all share in the 'germinative' word of God.

This development of a more rational, more subtle style of teaching was not restricted to public argument, to how the faith was represented in the forum of the world. Faith sought understanding within the Christian community also. Questions like, 'What is the nature of God?', 'Who is Jesus Christ?' began to be asked in a more distant, even academic way. Second-order questions they may have been, but they were of great importance. On them depended not only the coherence and credibility of Christian faith but also many practical consequences for its inner life and growth. There is a language of faith here, deeply different in tone and character from the first. The forms of the thought-world, the realm of meaning we can roughly label 'doctrine' maintains a cool and level distance from the experience of faith out of which it came.

From the start of Christian history, another element had been important, indeed essential, to the task of expressing and teaching the faith. The early Christians were 'faithful to the teaching of the apostles, to the brotherhood, to the breaking of bread and to the prayers'. Besides the storytelling and the preaching, besides the clearer formulation of the faith, that 'intolerable struggle with words and meanings', there was the act of formal and communal worship. Out of the breaking of bread grew the liturgy of the Church. Around the liturgy developed the catechumenate; a lengthy and systematic initiation of new members into the 'awe-inspiring mysteries of the faith'. In the catechumenate, the liturgy was a central strand, presenting these mysteries and punctuating the phases of initiation. The liturgy became a web of word and silence, of symbol and action, of movement, colour and music; a rich idiom of faith, many-sided, allusive and subtle. The underlying conviction of the catechumenate was that because of these qualities it could touch the 'awe-inspiring mysteries' tangentially but more really than could other idioms marked by greater simplicity or greater clarity.

In the gospel finally, in the faith essentially, there exist strong moral demands. Some specific actions are praised or condemned; generosity, fidelity, murder, adultery, theft, injustice. However, the moral tower of the gospel is tilted away from codes of behaviour; it speaks of virtues, of holiness, of the paradoxical morality of the Beatitudes. Its chief demand is for a change of heart, for a conversion to new priorities and fresh attitudes.

The life of the early Christian community, however, continued to be thick with specific moral questions. St Paul often had to answer these or to reprove kinds of behaviour which he perceived as incompatible with the gospel. A coherent moral system based on the tradition of faith was needed and has emerged over the centuries. Like those concerned to express clear doctrine, moralists turned to Greek philosophy, to its ethical theories and especially to the doctrine of natural law. This posited a law of nature, intended in God's creation which reason can perceive, and which can be grafted onto the moral impetus of the gospel. This development had the virtue of linking Christian morality with the ethical concern and argument of all humankind. Less happily, the assimilation of this moral philosophy into the tradition of faith proved difficult and often seemed precarious. What, it would be asked from time to time, has been assimilated to what? So there exists a language of faith which involves quite complex moral argument.

Language and languages

The tradition of Christian faith then moved in several directions. Christians continued to share the experience of faith and to draw others into perceiving it. They also formulated that experience using a number of literary, philosophical and symbolic vehicles. In speaking of these as 'languages of faith' I do not mean that they are like French and German: self-contained linguistic systems with distinctive vocabularies, grammar and syntax. They are, however, ways of speaking faith which are deeply different from each other in character and even in purpose. They have their own ways of thinking and working, even their own distinctive tests for truth. They represent different realms of Christian meaning. They add complications to Christian faith; complexities which stem, through the central doctrine of the Incarnation, from its commitment to history and humanity; to the long and unfinished conversation between faith and reason.

Von Hugel's dilemma contrasted the experience of faith with its formulations. All these languages of faith are, in some sense, formulated. But some of them tilt towards experience. They hark eloquently back to it and catch its echoes. They deal in the concrete and the vivid rather than the abstract and precise; like story in the complexity of human actions and affairs, like liturgy in the rich allusiveness of sign and symbol. To say this is not to say that they are undisciplined. But they depend more on the imagination that on the abstract reason, and live within its discipline.

The other two of the languages that I have mentioned, doctrine and moral discourse, work in formulations of a more radical kind; distanced from experience or at least representing experience 'recollected in tranquillity'. As we have seen and shall see further, they have their value, even their necessity.

Von Hugel's dilemma remains unresolved, a dilemma for all of us. To look at things in this way, however, throws some light on it. Things are rarely black and white. The experience of faith is difficult to formulate but not impossible. Formulations of faith can be dull and boring but need not be so. The different languages of faith should interact and nourish each other. But if this is to happen, they must be understood well and spoken fluently. Learning the languages of faith is an indispensable task.

Chapter 1

THE TRUTH OF IMAGINATION
The Language of Story

The preaching of the gospel and the life of the Church began with Peter's sermon at Pentecost. 'Men of Israel, listen to what I am going to say. Jesus the Nazarene was a man commended to you by God by the miracles and portents and signs that God worked through him when he was among you, as you all know. This man who was put into your power by the deliberate intention and foreknowledge of God, you took and had crucified by men outside the Law. You killed him but God raised him to life, freeing him from the pangs of Hades...' (Acts 2:22-24).

It is a sermon which establishes the form of the 'Kerygma', the message or preaching of the apostles; it shapes it in the form of a story. Peter recounts the events of Jesus' life (the teacher, the healer, the dead and risen one), goes on to appeal to the past (the one foretold) and to look to the future (repent, the age of the Messiah is come). To tell that story seemed the obvious thing to do. It was a way of teaching which reflected most closely his own vivid experience, which seemed to fulfil most immediately the call to 'make disciples of all the nations'. So story became the first of the languages of faith. Perhaps it is still the best but it is not the only voice in which teachers of the gospel have spoken. Our first question is: What is a story? Where does its power come from? Is it really the simple beginning, middle and end that it seems? Or does it have a lot of skins like an onion, a lot of dimensions of meaning? Who shall help us with this? Who shall tell us a good story?

Why, Charles Dickens of course. Here he is, spiritedly launching *Hard Times,* setting things in motion, setting, indeed, the cat among the pigeons. 'Girl number twenty unable to define a horse!' said Gradgrind, for the general behoof of all the little pitchers. 'Girl number twenty possessed of no facts in reference to one of the commonest of animals! Some boy's definition of a horse. Bitzer, Yours.' 'Quadruped. Graminivorous. Forty teeth, namely twenty-four grinders, four eye-teeth and twelve incisors. Sheds coat in the spring; in marshy countries, sheds hoofs too. Hoofs hard but requiring to be shod with iron. Age known by marks in mouth.' Thus (and much more) Bitzer. 'Now girl number twenty', said Mr Gradgrind, 'You know what a horse is'. Mr Gradgrind is the apostle of facts. 'Facts alone are wanted in life. Plant nothing else and root out everything else.'[1] Bitzer is his sinister disciple. Behind them lurks not only the flat world of facts and utilitarian philosophy but also the chilling shadow of Coketown and the dark Satanic mills. Girl number twenty is Sissy Jupe. She is a circus child and her people know all about horses though with a different kind of knowledge from Bitzer's. They have plenty of common sense but their lives are marked also by joy, spontaneity, affection and compassion. In this wonderful novel, Dickens sets out to resolve the conflict between these two worlds. His method is not to conduct an analysis or write political philosophy. He simply unrolls the events, and who can unroll events better than Dickens? Through the rise of Sissy, the downfall of Gradgrind, the sterile triumph of Bitzer, he leads the reader not to solutions or even judgements. What we come to at the end is recognition.

The question 'Who is my neighbour?' is, at first sight, not unlike the question 'What is a horse?' It could be answered in the manner of Bitzer: person, contiguous with interests and needs. It would be possible to filter out a definition in a timeless and disembodied mode. Jesus declined this prospect and began his answer, 'A man went down from Jerusalem to Jericho'. There has been much discussion about the structure and context of this famous story. However it is read, it seems certain that the force of the question was: 'How far does our responsibility for others extend; how far must we go in this duty of neighbourly love?' Jesus saw that that question would not be well answered, perhaps could not be answered at all through an abstract definition. His concern as a teacher was not with knowledge in Gradgrind's sense but rather with recognition; with the immediacy and conviction and personal certainty which that word implies.

Dickens begins his narrative with a light-hearted touch. But the themes he sets going are serious ones. It is similar to the way in which Beethoven sometimes introduces a symphony, with a phrase which seems at first hearing undistinguished, even pedestrian. But it turns out to have a great future. Its possibilities are not realised until the last note is played. The Book of Genesis also launches a story, even a drama. It tells of God's creation of the cosmos and of humankind. Men and women are God's creatures. Their sexual complementarity and fruitfulness are central to their lives and the life of the human race. They are given responsibility for the world, even, to some degree, power over it. For the use of this power they are answerable to God. Theirs is a moral world laced with motives, temptations, alternatives and choices. Although it is a happy world, human freedom can flaw, even shatter it. This is the start of a great story, of what D. H. Lawrence called 'a great confused novel... man alive not mere bits'.[2] Here are its elements, its constituents. Only as its events unfold will its possibilities be realised, its range of meanings emerge. The story continues now, the unfolding of numerous eras and cultures is necessary before it is complete. Unlike the Good Samaritan, it does not address an open question. But behind it lie a number of linked implicit questions which are in all our hearts. They are not questions which can be answered by definitions in the Gradgrind manner. They are questions which engage the imagination and the heart.

Do stories matter?

I have been making some large claims for stories. They address some deep questions in an indispensable way. There are some levels of truth and goodness which are accessible only to them. There are plenty of opposition witnesses who could be called to contest this case. The most eminent of them is Plato, who would not have storytellers or poets in his ideal republic.[3] He could see their attraction, but he believed they should be crowned with laurels and banished. He thought that fictions are a form of untruth. This was not because they ignore the checks and challenges of academic history. Rather it is because their ingredients are lodged in the world of sense. People, happenings, imagery, landscapes, houses are part of material reality; and the material world is a realm of illusions and mistakes. Truth is elsewhere. Truth is in a disembodied world of eternal and changeless forms. The artist is ensnared in the sense-world and draws us away from true understanding. Abstraction into a world of pure ideas is the condition of truth.

Plato has had plenty of supporters. Even Sir Philip Sidney in his 'Defence of Poesy'[4] offers a justification for poetry which is rather shamefaced. 'Poesy' is an attractive façade. Its grace and elegance is like sweet honey which can make palatable the bitter but medicinal rhubarb of morality. In this view poetry – and storytelling – is a decorative extra. But the real stuff is elsewhere. It is in moral principles. It is in metaphysics. In the history of the Christian Church also, such views are common enough. There are Christian Platonists by philosophical principle and method. There are those who are influenced by Plato's other-worldly view of truth in more oblique ways. They are wary of sense, of the fleshly, of the contingent. They look back and think that the only time in which the Church enthusiastically wedded the arts was the era of the Renaissance popes. And look what corruption ensued! The artist – including the poet and the storyteller – should be kept at arm's length.

Plato was a great philosopher but he was also profoundly wrong. To envisage a disembodied world where reality subsists in eternal ideas is neither necessary nor helpful. Truth exists in this world of sense and experience and in what the human mind makes of it. We may look afresh at what the storyteller makes of it. She clearly makes something of it. What is presented is not a buzzing, booming confusion. It is not, or need not be, a simple re-presentation of events in the interest of vividness or sensation. At its best, a story orders and illuminates experience. In its web of character, event and image, it catches the elusive fish of meaning. How does it do this? D. H. Lawrence, in his lively defence of the novel, may put us on the right road.

> …I am a novelist. And being a novelist, I consider myself superior to the saint, the scientist, the philosopher and the poet, who are all great masters of different bits of man alive, but never get the whole hog.
>
> The novel is the one bright book of life. Books are not life. They are only tremulations on the ether. But the novel as a tremulation can make the whole man alive tremble. Which is more than poetry, philosophy, science or any other book-tremulation can do.

'Make the whole man alive tremble.' Lawrence's point is that when we separate some area of experience – logical reasoning say, or empirical observation, or even mystical vision – and lift it out of the whole, we have something which is convenient to deal with but dead. The word is a medium which is subtle and flexible enough to take up the whole of experience, order it and present it so that the reader trembles with the shock of recognition. How can stories do this?

Achilles and the tortoise

The tortoise challenged Achilles to a race. He asked for a yard's start and was certain he would win. He reasoned in this way. By the time Achilles has made up the yard's start I will have moved ahead, let us say, by two inches. By the time he has covered the two inches, I will have gone ahead again – perhaps by only half an inch, but still, Achilles has to make that up. By the time he has, I shall be ahead again. By the time he reaches any point on the course I shall have advanced beyond it – perhaps by an infinitesimally small distance but enough to keep me in the lead. So I am bound to win the race. Put your money on me.

Within his own framework of thought, the tortoise is right. If distance is a series of points, then whenever Achilles reaches a point, the tortoise will have gone beyond it. Alas, the tortoise lost the race and all his supporters their money. Where had he gone wrong? It was in thinking of distance as a series of points in some way separable. Distance is a continuum. In it, speed is a factor of greater importance than position. In a race, it is how fast you move, not where you are, which determines who wins.

Similarly experience is not a series of points. It is not a set of discrete units which can be separated out, at least not without damage to the whole. This is why, as Lawrence rightly said, the story can win experience as Achilles won the race and make us tremble. For narrative is the image of duration. A story is the only medium which can present experience still within its vital element of time. Stories begin, openly or implicitly, 'Once upon a time!' 'They lived happily ever after' ritually announces the end of the sequence of events. Even if the ending is inconsequential, still a line of finality can be drawn. The story is told. It is complete. 'Only connect', is E. M. Forster's advice to the novelist, 'only connect'. Yet in the duration of the story, the events are not placed in an arbitrary line, nor do they simply follow each other by the measure of clock or calendar. The connections in the narrative involve cause and consequence, hidden motives, new facets of character, revelations, crises. The sequence carries us forward not only through a curiosity to know what happens next; but also by a curiosity about why and how our experience is patterned in the way it is.

There is another factor which lends stories their power. We are drawn into their flow as we can never be drawn into the flow of a logical argument, however spirited. We identify positively or negatively with the characters. We experience their fate vicariously. It is this involvement which justifies the use of the word 'recognition' to describe the effect which an important story has on its readers. Nothing is learned which can be held at arm's length. It is learning of the heart and of the imagination. When we 'see' the solution of a difficult crossword clue, what follows is an inward chuckle of intellectual satisfaction. A moment of recognition is quite a different experience and sometimes quite a disturbing one which rises from deeper roots. The 'tremulations' from which it comes may involve our feelings deeply. Not that feelings are separate from concepts and logic as black is the opposite of white. They are parts of a single act, the apprehension of the heart. Yet many kinds of discourse leave them untouched. The story, however, enfolds feelings and carries them to a new place as it makes the whole man alive tremble.

A story can create a new order in consciousness, can do this, Coleridge writes, because it works 'not only by the intellect but by the whole concourse of mental powers, of thought, feeling, purpose and imagination'. He continues, 'deep thinking is attainable only by a man of deep feeling and all truth is a species of revelation'. Coleridge is not using the word 'revelation' in a strict theological way (though what he says has plenty of theological echoes). In its more everyday sense 'revelation' pairs, in an illuminating way, with 'recognition'. For we recognise something not with an agile mental somersault, but because it is there, because it is in some way given to us. Coleridge wishes to reassert the value of contemplative wisdom ('All is gift') against the instrumental analytic intellect, against the world of Bitzer, Bentham and the Enlightenment.

Stories and truth

Jesting Pilate was neither the first nor the last to ask, 'What is Truth?', and not to stay for an answer. It is certainly not a question which rings in the same register as 'What is a horse?', or 'What is a triangle?', or even, 'What is democracy?' The physicist in a laboratory, the mathematician in the study, the historian in a library, the judge in her court all seek truth. Yet their methods are as diverse as their outcomes. These stand on different grounds; some are said to be beyond a shadow of doubt, some beyond a reasonable doubt, some highly probable, able to hold their ground until a better version is produced. One picture of truth as a quality of human expression is that there is a core of 'hard' truths (say the fruits of empirical investigation or mathematical logic). These can be confidently held with absolute certainty. But there is a wider range of 'soft' truths, the fruit of less exact methods. These can be received with varying degrees of probability or opinion. This seems a questionable picture. An alternative one is that in our studies, our discourse, our quest, we play various 'language games', the game of science, the game of history, the game of ethics. Each game has its rules. If it is seriously played, it has its truth-conditions. This is a less tidy, less monolithic picture. But to those who have stood in the waiting-room of truths for a long time, it breathes the breath of reality. What are the truth-conditions of stories?

Many people have to assess the truth of stories. In a court of law it is the business of judge and jury to listen to the accounts of the same events as given by different witnesses, to hear the presentations made by counsel and to decide what the truth of the matter is. Of course, the court is not engaging with any complex idea of truth but trying more simply to discover what happened and perhaps make an assessment of the intentions of the defendant. There are many stories, including stories of faith, which do not attempt to describe events which happened in the real world. We have all heard sad stories of children who run away from home. But there is no reason to think that Jesus had a particular case in mind when he told the story of the prodigal son. The fact that the story is always called a parable indicates that it is not concerned to describe actual events. It has a different point. Still, the workings of a court of law does give us one helpful clue. This is that a court has to put together and evaluate the stories of a number of witnesses. Each witness has a different point of view. One is perhaps a relative of the accused, one a companion of the victim, one an accidental bystander. Stories are told from a particular point of view, against a particular horizon, within a particular perspective. In assessing their truth, the viewpoint must be seen and must be taken into account. Stories have a context. They do not exist in a vacuum. They do not run wild in the desert. Their context must be taken into account both in understanding their meaning and in judging their truth.

Each of the witnesses in our case saw the drama from a different angle. Some had only a glimpse of it or had poor eyesight. Some saw what happened clearly but had no idea of the background, the character of the actors, the relationships that might be involved. Some will tell partisan stories for they have the interests of the defendant at heart. Their bias may not lead them to falsify the facts. There are ways of telling stories, through rearrangement, through emphasis, through a choice of words which slants them in a particular direction, in which they are interpreted and so, perhaps, judged. So they all tell different stories. Sometimes these stories converge into a single, clear narrative. Often they do not. Then it is the task of counsel to iron out contradictions and to weave a coherent narrative which is favourable to her client. She tells yet another story which the court must judge as it reaches a verdict.

The 'viewpoint' of a story, then, may consist of partial

knowledge, restricted vision, conscious or unconscious bias. A smart barrister will soon unmask the viewpoint and go at least some way towards uncovering the truth of the events which actually happened. But stories which do not purport to record actual events are a different case. They will not yield their truth to the tactics of sharp legal minds nor to courtroom discipline. Are they to be ruled out of court, banished from the Republic of Truth in the manner of Plato? Is fiction no more than fantasy? No, stories do embody important truths, indeed truths which cannot be expressed in any other way, cannot be reduced to a set of propositions. Discriminating among them, establishing their truth, is certainly no easy task. Let us at least try to see how it can be approached.

First, just as witnesses have viewpoints, so makers of stories have purposes. These may be conscious and practical. A story may be told as a warning, a call to change one's ways. 'Look how events have consequences' it might say. 'Look to it!' Jesus' parable of the sheep and the goats at the Last Judgment should probably be read that way. It is a call to repent. It is not a foretelling of things that will literally happen, a 'vision of judgment' in Byron's sense. If it is taken that way, it is misunderstood. Another story may be told to express a paradoxical truth. In Jesus' parable of the mustard seed, the kingdom is a tiny seed but has a potential for growth. Surely it will prove to be some vast and splendid Titan of a tree. But no. What will appear will be a substantial shrub and (a touch of irony?) the birds of the air will shelter in its branches. It is the most important thing in the world. But do not expect grandeur! A storyteller's purpose may, however, be less consciously planned. She may slip into the rhythms of an existing form of writing. Aesop found the fable, a common-enough type of story with a straightforward moral, and fitted his gifts into it. The picaresque novel was a common enough form in which the hero or anti-hero travelled constantly and had a series of disconnected adventures. Dickens saw its possibilities and took it up in *The Pickwick Papers*. By the time he reached *Hard Times* it no longer suited his purposes. He needed a different and more individual style.

The purpose of stories, their 'literary form', has an important bearing on this truth. If they are wrongly thought to be recording facts or foretelling the future, they will be misunderstood and wrongly judged. To identify the form and purpose of a story is not, of course, a guarantee of truth. It is not even a real criterion. But it is an indispensable condition. It sets up a framework of meaning within which judgements of truth can be made. How shall we go forward?

Cautiously. We play different language-games, we move in different realms of meaning. Valid tests for truth are different in each of them. T. W. Tilley in his extremely helpful book[5] offers a number of tests or criteria which might be used to weigh the truth of stories. He notes first of all that we use a number of words and phrases which are closely connected with truth but do not treat it as a sharp dividing line as between black and white. So, 'a likely story!' is a dismissive phrase which indicates that an account does not fit in with our experience of what commonly happens in life. To describe a story as 'exaggerated' does not quite say that it is untrue. Rather it says that the story contains some features which make us suspicious. There are tests which we apply to stories, and Tilley draws out and exemplifies several. Let us look at two of these.

Firstly, a story may be true in that it reveals to us something fresh. We say 'how true that is!'; it is the opposite of the implied dismissal in 'a likely story!' It is the acceptance, not of a new fact which can be squirreled away in our store of knowledge; but of a truth which is seen with the heart and known along the pulses. It is an acceptance very different from 'seeing the point' of an argument. We acknowledge the force of an argument as we bow to a checkmate in chess. 'How true that is!' accepts, 'with a fling of the heart', a revelation of meaning and value which compels the heart though it frequently goes against the grain. Revelations have a strong feel of the 'given'. They are not particularly sought after, and they are not always welcome. Because they are new and challenging, they are frequently quite unnerving.

In speaking to the crowds about John the Baptist, Jesus tells the tiny, haunting story of the children in the market-place. John is in prison, his mission wrecked on the rocks of indifference and betrayal. Jesus feels in himself both the resistance and the fickle enthusiasm of the people. They have no ears to hear, they 'refuse to repent'. To what will he compare them? To the children shouting to each other in the market-place:

> We have piped to you
> and you would not dance.
> We have mourned to you
> and you would not weep.[6]

For John came neither eating nor drinking, and they say, 'He is possessed'. The Son of Man came, eating and drinking, and they say, 'Look, a glutton and a drunkard, a friend of tax-collectors and sinners!' Perhaps the children piped for money. Certainly they did it expecting a response. The moment of recognition which the story leads to is, alas, a revelation of the hardness and heaviness of the human heart, of our resistance to truth, of our endless capacity for rationalisation.

Secondly, in a story we look for coherence. We look for a consistent fictional world which does not contradict itself in fact or value or feeling. Of course, a serious story does contain variety and often (as in *Hard Times*) the clash of irreconcilable visions and values. But these are held together in a single emotional and moral pattern. A true story does not espouse both ruthlessness and compassion. Nor does it rhetorically approve or condemn. It weaves them into a web of event and character whose imaginative coherence forms a horizon of judgement. Though we expect characters to be consistent we do not expect them to be unchanging. If they do not change, like Mrs Micawber whose 'I will never desert Mr Micawber' was her totality, we call them flat; more cartoons or caricatures than characters. However, we expect the development of a character to be consistent. Except in the case of Dr Jekyll and Mr Hyde we do not accept a radical fracture and the appearance of a new character like a genie from a bottle. Mr Gradgrind, for instance, changes profoundly. He is broken and reformed. Yet we are able to sense the germ of humanity and affection even in his most ruthless days. The character is, we say, credible.

With rather less confidence we may look for coherence between a story and the general run of our experience, our understanding of the world. We do this tentatively because stories rarely slot into the web of our understanding comfortably, like the last piece into a jigsaw puzzle. Indeed, as we have seen, a good story reveals and frequently jolts; and may be summarily dismissed, for that reason, as 'a likely story!' A modern reader comes across the Creation story in Genesis and dismisses it as primitive fantasy. This may be because she inhabits a very different story; perhaps it is the 'Enlightenment' story of triumphant reason, omniscient science and the onward march of evolution. Or it may be that the reader is half-consciously reducing the story to a set of facts and propositions. If the story is seen as a myth which seeks not to chronicle events but to express a few crucial religious truths, then the reduction to propositions may disappear and the reader's own story be challenged.

Consider the phrase, 'telling it like it is'. This is usually meant as an accolade. The story is realistic. Nothing is romanticised, nothing glamorised. No deep significance is read into it. It has the griminess and grittiness of raw experience. Life is nasty, brutish and short, and the story effectively expresses this. The reader here also inhabits his own story. Perhaps it is a post-modern one, suspicious of large generalisations of idealism, of the intrusion into experience of broad perspectives. His reaction to the story of the Good Samaritan might be: sure, people get mugged and beaten up. But it doesn't work out like that – the oil and wine, the personal care, the money. People drive on. Expect at best the clinical, commercial care of paramedics. The story dominant in a person's life is resistant to stories which query it; in this the dismissive word would be not unlikely but unrealistic.

Quite often, our own story makes us opaque to the story of others; as a person brought up in and formed by a strong culture frequently finds a different culture alien, perhaps threatening. Forced to live in it or relate to it they feel uprooted and anxious. So, coherence with the rest of our experience and understanding seems a shaky test for truth; unless the story concerned is a soothing anodyne. Yet there is something in it. 'How very true that is' may indeed acknowledge the jarring revelation of something new. Yet the openness to a new vision, to a reorientation of our understanding, does not come from nowhere. It arises out of the coherence of our own story which contains not only strength to resist but also flexibility to perceive. A story can be a prison cell. It can also be a road to freedom. A significant story (Enlightenment, modern, post-modern) tells itself at a deeper level than surfaces. It can enable us to see that a foreign story is coherent with the range of our experience at a level deeper than familiar immediacies. It is the level of our understanding of how the world wags, of the way things turn out, of what is important, what is authentic, what is wise. Stories from a different culture, stories which startle by their otherness, stories which shock, can sometimes compel also. They can pierce the protective carapace of our own story and shake in us the structures of likelihood.

These considerations – that the truth of stories may be tested in so far as they are in some way revelatory, in some way coherent – may help to show that judging the truth of stories, though a far cry from the test-tube, is not a hopeless task. Certainly there are other approaches which enable us to detect the pulse of truth. However, we have to meet the objection that what is discussed here is not truth at all but effectiveness. We are showing only that stories work. They catch the reader's attention, engage her interest, shock her, make her think. But this could be achieved whether the teller is a careful diarist or a whopping liar.

Well, to go backwards a little, 'truth' and 'effectiveness' are connected words, just as 'exaggerated' and 'false' are not opposed to each other but rather represent gradations on the same scale. Truth is not simple and uniform but is embodied differently in the several realms of meaning within which we live. Storytelling belongs, whether in a simple or sophisticated way, in the realm of the arts. If we look there we may be further enlightened. We might start from Suzanne Langer's helpful distinction between discursive and presentational forms. The former presents its offering as a logical structure; premises, evidence, conclusion. The latter presents its case (as in a picture or a story) all in one, through a single mesh of subtly interrelated elements. To create such a unity is the work of the imagination.

The truth of the imagination

> I am certain of nothing but of the holiness of the heart's affections and the truth of imagination.[7]

Keats writes this at a time of loneliness and loss. These are the fragments which he will shore against his ruins, the 'holiness of the heart's affection', the 'truth of the imagination'. Is this mere poetic fantasy, frothing on the surface of life? Is it more than a manifestation of the Romantic agony setting feeling against reason, imagination against logical argument? It is much more than that. Keats' holiness is not a fugitive and cloistered virtue. It is to be sought in the heart's affections, in the world of *eros* rather than *logos,* in the world of uncalculating love, generosity and faithfulness. Keats pairs holiness and truth. It is a theme which echoes the Gospel. Jesus prays that his followers may be 'consecrated in the truth', made holy in it. And he urges that generous self-giving love is the sure path to holiness and therefore is a pre-condition of truth. Keats also pairs the heart's affections with the imagination. Both manifest the unifying creativity of the human spirit; the one bonding persons, the other fusing into a pattern the multifoliate variety of the world, 'that love which moves the sun and the other stars'.

This link between imagination and truth is in one way surprising. For we often use the word imagination to mean the opposite of truth. We console an invalid by saying 'Oh, it's just your imagination playing tricks'. Keats was not philosopher enough to unravel the complex meaning of the word. But Coleridge was. He was a person who experienced the collapse of the ordered world of public certainties reflected in Chaucer and Shakespeare and in a different way by Dr Johnson and Pope. He sensed also the beginnings of modern life, a world of 'nervous individual consciousness, fluid categories and collapsing order'. He recognised the need for a fresh, creative expression of an experience becoming increasingly disorderly. He sought a unity which would not depend on a common ideology. Order in consciousness was, for him, a work of the imagination. Let us follow him a little way as he unpacks the word. Here is the start of it in a famous passage from *Biographia Literaria*. 'The imagination[8] then, I consider either as primary or secondary. The primary imagination I hold to be the living power and prime agent of all human perception, and as a repetition in the finite mind of the eternal act of creation in the infinite I AM. The secondary imagination I consider as an echo of the former, co-existing with the conscious will yet still as identical with the primary in the *mind* of its agency and differing only in *degree,* and in the *mode* of its operation. It dissolves, diffuses, dissipates, in order to re-create; or where this process is impossible, yet still at all events, it struggles to realise and to unify. It is essentially *vital,* even as all objects (as objects) are essentially fixed and dead.

'*Fancy,* on the contrary, has no other counters to play with but fixities and definites. The fancy is, indeed, no other than a mode of memory emancipated from the order of time and space; while it is blended with, and modified by that empirical phenomenon of the will which we express by the word Choice. But equally with the ordinary memory the Fancy must receive all its material ready-made from the law of association.'

In this famous piece, Coleridge certainly takes a high view of the imagination. It works powerfully on experience and on intellectual traditions. It is analytic in that it 'dissolves, diffuses, dissipates', probing and refocusing experience. But its purpose is neither destructive nor sceptical. It is to bring into being fresh formulations of the experience or the tradition. These (like their maker) have an essential vitality as against mere objects or mere concepts which are 'essentially fixed and dead'. The similarity with Newman's idea of the development of the Christian 'idea' in history and theology is striking. This 'changes in order to remain the same'. If it fails to do this, its formulations turn into relics, fixed and dead, like flies elegantly preserved in amber.

The nature of the imagination appears more sharply when it is set against that of fancy. The word 'fancy' (we get the feel of it, more strongly, in the adjective 'fanciful') is essentially superficial and decorative, like the marzipan on the cake. It deals only with fixities and definites. All that can be done with them is to shift them into different patterns on the board; as in the old ecclesiastical joke that to undertake Church reform is to shift around the deckchairs on the *Titanic.* The deep difference between imagination and fancy is embodied in a sharp, illuminating way through the distinction between metaphor and simile. Both involve laying alongside each other different things, ideas, or qualities in such a way that language becomes more colourful and communication more luminous. As children we were taught to use these comparisons often; otherwise our language would be flat, no-one would listen to us and we would get poor marks in our compositions as well. So, instead of saying about Richard I, 'he fought bravely', we should say, 'he fought like a lion'. Thus, a new presence appears in the mind's eye and our reader's understanding of the King's bravery acquires vitality and force. We were also taught (and I much regret that the phrase was so catchy and proved so memorable): 'Metaphor is simile with the "like" left out'. You might say, 'he was a lion in the fight' and so be more direct and immediate and perhaps also save a few words. I now believe this statement to be badly mistaken and deeply misleading; and that when we learn to use metaphors, we are learning something much more important and something genuinely creative.

Consider this well-known image from T. S. Eliot's 'Love Song of J. Alfred Prufrock':

> The yellow fog that rubs its back upon the window-
>   panes,
> The yellow smoke that rubs its muzzle on the window-
>   panes,
> Licked its tongue into the corners of the evening
> Lingered upon the pools that stand in drains,
> Let fall upon its back the soot that falls from chimneys
> Slipped by the terrace, made a sudden leap,
> And seeing that it was a soft October night,
> Curled once about the house, and fell asleep.

Adherents of the school of 'simile with the "like" left out' would argue that what Eliot is saying is: 'the autumn evening was rather like a cat'. But immediately we see that this is a ludicrous distortion, that what is occurring in the poem is something totally different. The poet is fusing together the sinuous, insinuating animality of the cat, with the depression of an autumn ('fall') evening; and also with the squalor, the meaningless and debilitating triviality of life ('drains', 'soot', 'chimneys'); also with a sense of being hopelessly overcome by that, a theme orchestrated in the rest of the poem.

> I have heard the mermaids singing, each to each.
> I do not think that they will sing to me.

The poet is creating a single image of real depth and power – a metaphor.

Metaphors of faith

A metaphor then, fuses elements which are diverse, separate and weak into unities which are fresh and powerful. One of the purposes which the language of story serves is the creation of metaphors of faith. In Christian life, in preaching and teaching, many different elements have to be brought together: reason and experience; biblical tradition and philosophy; Church teaching and contemporary circumstance; history, culture and perennial truth. In our minds, quite often, these things lie about in a kind of holy jumble; connected here, at odds there, elsewhere linked by some logical artifice. Of course in all minds, in all sensibilities these are cracks, tensions, 'dissociations'. Still, a faith with real strength and vitality is upheld by a few luminous and life-giving metaphors which deeply unify these diverse elements.

The word 'metaphor' does not get a universally good press. We often hear 'just a metaphor' spoken in the same tone of voice as 'a mere story' or 'it is only your imagination'. The presupposition behind these remarks is that metaphors, like stories, serve only to illustrate, decorate, exemplify, make vivid a truth which is arrived at by some other route. It is an example of the view which supposes that these are 'hard truths' which can be verified experimentally or deductively, which are 'ontologically the case'. We have seen that this is over-simple. Truth is established differently within our several realms of meaning. It is true that it is clearer and easier to discern in some of them, but it not thereby 'harder', more profound or more reliable. As Coleridge argues, the function of the imagination is to fuse very disparate realities into new patterns of meaning. Because of their unified complexity, their truth will be established more obliquely and by approaching them (as we have seen with stories) not from one, but from several different angles.

Salvation history

Nowadays, modernity envelops us and history is a fading song. Of old, the resources for wisdom and education were found in the classical past. Now the present is the vivid foreground of our lives though we peer tentatively into the future. Yet our personal history often leaves us deeply marked. Nations, too, bear their history like an inheritance, sometime a heartening one, sometimes tragic. History has fallen on hard times, is seen often just as a means of 'disowning the past'. Yet history offers understanding, even sometimes a kind of wisdom. It may be a bondage ('victims of their history'). It may also serve to free us from enslavement to the single optic of the present.

Academic history most often has a sophisticated and careful concern for accuracy, for establishing the course of events. It is cautious about cause and consequence, about judgements of character, about recurring patterns. Yet there are historians who take a more committed, even a prophetic view of their task. Whig history had its standpoint and constructed its story in the light of that. There was an evolutionary history which envisaged the human lot as steadily improving, with occasional lapses; of which sad illusion we have mostly disabused ourselves. There is a black history and a feminist history in which values and ideals, hopes and grievances are prominent themes in the fugue that is woven. Such histories are not necessarily less true than supposedly 'letting the facts speak for themselves', than supposedly 'telling it like it is'; unless of course, they can be convicted of positive dishonesty or of carelessness.

Salvation history is the story of the presence and action of God's saving grace in the cosmos and in human affairs. It is a story of faith, for only faith perceives that reality. It is not therefore, academic history in the sense of shying away from larger patterns of meaning. It does not draw on factual records only but includes fictional stories, for these also have their truth. Nor does it arrange events only according to the drab effluxion of time. Consider, for example, the presentation of the genealogy of Christ in Matthew's Gospel. Its arrangement in three sets of fourteen generations – from Abraham to David, from David to the Babylonian exile, from Babylon to Christ – is not really concerned to count the generations or list the facts exactly. It seeks to present a symmetry, an order and pattern in events. It seeks to present history not as an untidy, rambling network of human destinies but rather a pattern shaped in the rhythms of grace.

The reason why story, why salvation history, is the first language of faith, is a simple one. It is that Christianity began and continues, not primarily a philosophical system but a historical fact. The word of God became, not as an institution, nor a set of concepts, but flesh. God's revelation is made in history, for history is 'the lengthened shadow of a man'. It is made, therefore, subject to the laws of human growth. Its climactic event is led up to, foreshadowed, pursued. This event does not disclose its full meaning at once. A person came, loved, taught, suffered, died and rose again. It would take the unrolling of epochs and centuries, the rise and fall of cultures, nations and languages to unfold the full impact of this happening.

Scripture as story

D. H. Lawrence's description of the Bible as a 'great confused novel' may not find much favour with Scripture scholars. There is a great deal of narrative in the Bible, but there are other kinds of writing too, 'wisdom', theological instruction, mysticism, allegory. Biblical writers have their personal viewpoints, work within their culture, slot into established literary forms. All the same, a novel can contain such elements without losing its essential narrative drive. Think of Tolstoy's reflections on history in *War and Peace*. Think how *The Brothers Karamazov* manages to contain the huge parable of the Grand Inquisitor; it stands there, a mountainous story, outside the flow of events yet without any sense of a digression; kneaded into the deeper rhythms which move below the surface. Similarly the Bible contains many forms of writing without losing its essential narrative thrust.

A good story, especially a 'huge confused' one usually contains sub-plots. Sometimes these simply provide comic relief. Sometimes they mirror, at a different social level, the main theme of the tale. But sometimes, like a counterpoint, they run against it. In Shakespeare's problem plays there is no single vision. It is a drama of the unresolved, of the catches and ambivalences of life. In the Scriptures we find this too. It is the story of God's grace. But that grace embodied, made flesh among us, does not appear a monolithic system. A striking illustration of this fact, of the presence of theme and counter-subject, is the interplay, in the Scriptures, of myth and parable.

'Myth' is a word which might carry a theological health-warning. As 'telling stories' sometimes means telling lies, so myth sometimes means falsification. Yet myth has a positive meaning. It is a story which embodies important truths about the meaning and value of life; it expresses these, not in a philosophical and abstract way, but with the sharp particularity of a narrative which does not fade into vague generalities. Yet the events and persons carry a meaning beyond themselves. It is a case of 'not this or that particular man but mankind'. Myths are called 'foundational' when the history and culture of a nation or group rests on them; when they are the source of an established way of seeing and understanding the world and also of the values and virtues which form the basis of public morality. King Arthur and his knights at the Round Table provided the basis for a style of courtly life, in the themes of semi-divine royalty, fealty and gallantry (also with its darker side). The Scriptures can be seen as the foundational myth of Christian life, establishing its main themes: God's creation and saving love, human triumph and brokenness, the redemptive work of Christ in the new creation. It is on this story that the common life of faith is founded.

Yet a strong shared life easily slips into being as an ideology. Visions turn into rules. Life in a strong framework of meaning easily degenerates into deadening correctness. Jesus, living in, accepting and completing an ancient heritage, was well aware of this. Hence many of his stories were parables. For a parable is the contradiction of a myth, its gadfly, its menacing shadow. In the story of the Good Samaritan, the representatives of established virtue pass by on the other side. It is the enemy, the outsider, who emerges as hero. The established view of things is challenged and subverted. The Scriptures do establish a foundational myth but they also strike the radical note of prophecy. Although they bring the strong support of a life of settled purpose, theirs is not a soothing rhythm. Read with an open mind and heart they do not induce but constantly prick complacency.

In the Body of Christ
The Scriptures are normative in Christian life, both in our personal span and in the larger perspective. The Church values and venerates them as 'she venerates the Lord's body'. Nevertheless, salvation history does not end with the Apocalypse any more than revelation ends with the death of the last apostle. Salvation history continues in the Body of Christ. This most honourable of titles is given to the Church, for she is an organism rather than an organisation; her task is to continue Christ's work, to teach God's truth, to embody and share his grace.

The history of the Church differs from the Scriptures in so far as it falls more substantially within the domain of formal history. There is not the same necessity for complex interpretation in terms of literary and cultural forms and standpoints. On the other hand, Church history is not entirely 'telling it like it is'. The salvation-historian has a standpoint; sees in the Church God's enlightening and healing grace committed to a community of fragile human persons. Inevitably, the vitality, the persistence and the failures of the Church are seen in that light. Nor is the history of the Church innocent of literary forms. For example, the lives of the saints are often written to a formula. They accept a blueprint of sanctity, possibly a time-conditioned, transient one; perhaps that holiness consists of miracles, ecstasies and asceticism. The human life of the saint is crammed into this Procrustean bed and the story loses its power. For the power rests in the presence of the whole 'man alive' which sets the tree of experience trembling. The lives of the saints are epics, like the stories of Judith and Samson in the Bible. In them the ideals and values commonly held are heroically vindicated in an individual life. But these values develop and mature, they are sometimes distorted. The ideal of sanctity changes, is sometimes other-worldly, sometimes incarnate. Because of this we need new saints to look up to; and we need to perceive the human reality of their lives: 'heart speaks to heart'.

Despite these elements of interpretation, despite the imaginative demands they make ('creating new metaphors of faith'), the requirement of truthfulness in recounting the history of the Church is more straightforward and therefore more black-and-white. The teller of this tale is vulnerable to bias; not through deliberate falsification but rather through the devices of arrangement and emphasis. There is a special danger of being drawn into the rhetoric of the large sweep, 'the faith is Europe and Europe is the faith'.

History can be large or small, it can be inner or outer. It can focus on external events, particularly those which shape our lives, and on the persons who, at least on the surface, are their initiators. 'Official' histories are often written. These have an 'official view'. They are written from the heart of the group whose destiny they chronicle. Consequently they concentrate attention on the views and actions of the leaders of the group concerned. Official histories have an official standpoint. Church history is open to the temptation of officialdom. It can slip easily into dealing with important events only, the actions and policies of group leaders, in this case of popes and bishops. Those decisions do of course shape the life of the Church, yet a salvation history constructed round them turns out to be a pretty thin porridge. It is the history of an organisation rather than an organism. The life of the Body of Christ contains also many prophetic voices and these, not infrequently, meet official disapproval. Yet the test of time may show that they have been the authentic voice of Catholic tradition.

Official history, moreover, is conducted at a level which misses another indispensable sector of salvation history. This is the common life and understanding of the faithful, all of whom 'share in understanding and handing on revealed truth. They have received the anointing of the Holy Spirit who instructs them and guides them into all truth'. Salvation history is a language which expresses and communicates faith. The tradition of faith often appears both more vividly and more truly in the common life of a community than in its official formulations.

Within this common life, finally, stands the telling of our personal stories, that 'faith-sharing' which is nowadays so frequent and so valued as an element both in evangelisation and catechesis. Recounting our personal history in faith, more than in other matters, costs. 'Nothing requires a greater intellectual heroism than to see one's own personal equation written out.' In telling our story we are especially vulnerable to both self-delusion and self-dramatisation. We may not be required, may not even be able to tell the whole truth. Yet honesty is all. Glibness, the sense that experience has crystallised into a set of fixed and final formulas, is mortal. Telling one's story, especially face-to-face ('heart speaks to heart'), has great power to compel. Yet the power to compel can be seductive. Like all power it may corrupt. There is something of an intoxication in the feeling of swaying others – the hushed attention, the intent eyes, the winged words. Perhaps it will be a flash in the pan, a 'utopia of the immediate', kindling quickly but already a dying ember. It is necessary to find ways of so telling one's faith story that it appears for what it is; as an episode in salvation history, an embodiment of something which happens in the whole community, a part of the larger history of faith into which others may, along this little road, be drawn.

On the road to Emmaus

Many people return to the story of the journey to Emmaus again and again; and find it, even after many years, a wellspring bubbling with fresh life. It is a factual story, no allegory or parable, yet in its structure and flow, in the manner of its telling, it is far more than a record of events. It is one of those stories told by St Luke which concern a journey and a road. The road itself is a prominent feature in the story, unlike the roads travelled by Pickwick or Don Quixote, which simply link disparate adventures. It is not that the road, tarmacadam or cobblestones or mud and dust is evoked. Rather, as in the old film *La Strada*, the road is present and insistent in its sense of directive thrust and purposeful travel, in its possibilities for unforeseen encounter, for change of scene and mood, in its movement towards exile and alienation and, equally, towards homecoming and peace.

On this road the first two characters appear, lonely figures against a sombre horizon. One, Cleopas, is identified, as is their destination, Emmaus; to give a certain sharp particularity to a story which might otherwise dissolve in clouds of mystery. They are not heroic figures. This is no epic. They walk disconsolate and disappointed. They have had the experience of Jesus and can speak about it coherently, even eloquently. Yet it is as an experience that no longer makes sense, for the hopes they thought fulfilled in it have been dashed. They have had the experience but missed the meaning. There has been talk of a Resurrection but probably this is nothing more than old wives' tales.

A third traveller joins them – overtaking their melancholy pace or perhaps at a crossroads. The traveller is Jesus, yet, like Mary Magdalen, like the apostles in their boat, they fail to recognise him. The risen Lord is present but it is now the era of faith rather than immediacy; the time for seeing through a glass darkly, the time of signs and moments of illumination. Jesus travels with them and begins to share their concerns and they are open in their sadness, 'We had hoped that he was the one…'. Jesus begins to re-read their experience in the light of the Scriptures, 'O Foolish men and slow of heart to believe… was it not necessary that the Christ should suffer…?' As he conducts this re-reading their spirits begin to lift and their hopes to re-kindle: 'Were not our hearts burning within us…?' The road is carrying them towards new faith, it is carrying them towards recognition. The words 'knowledge' and 'understanding', 'recognition' and 'reading' all come from the same Greek root. Through re-reading in the light of Scripture, knowledge and understanding shuffle themselves into new patterns and the moment of recognition is close.

They reach Emmaus and the third traveller makes as though to go on. It is not a conventional gesture like a dramatic aside which the other characters pretend not to hear. We can avoid the denouement if we wish; and not only through malice but equally through a lack of openheartedness. The travellers respond: 'Stay with us, it is towards evening'. Darkness, paradoxically, is gathering in the womb of light. They sit at table to share a meal as they have shared a journey. To be a companion – *cum pane* – is to be a sharer of bread. Shortly the full meaning of companionship will come to light.

'They recognised him; and he vanished...'. The moment of truth is also the moment of darkness. Yet it is the 'deep and dazzling darkness' of living faith. Their hopes recovered, they rise immediately and return to Jerusalem to tell the others how they recognised him in the breaking of bread. It is the beginning of the Church, its testimony and its mission.

'Never trust the teller, trust the tale.' Storytellers on the whole would not get up out of the narrative and give us an explanation of its meaning. In a good story truth is embodied, not preached. St Luke observes this principle. All the same, at this moment we are very aware of the teller's perspective. He belongs to a community where the Eucharist is familiar and central. He creates his story in the light of that. The liturgy of the word is a re-reading of life in the light of Scripture. It breaks in its way the bread of Christ's risen presence. The breaking of bread itself brings that dawning perception to its fulfilment. Here is the real presence of Christ who is for most of our lives a hooded traveller, a shaded presence at our side.

In the story the writer creates a compelling metaphor of faith; bringing together person and incident, recognition and belief, apostolic commitment and liturgical practice in a unified image. It is a singularly luminous example of the power of story as a language of faith.

Chapter 2

'A BLESSED RAGE FOR ORDER'
The Language of Doctrine

> Oh! Blessed rage for order, pale Ramon,
> The maker's rage to order words of the sea,
> Words of the fragrant portals, dimly-starred,
> And of ourselves and of our origins,
> In ghostlier demarcations, keener sounds.[1]

The title of this chapter comes from a poem by Wallace Stevens, 'The Idea of Order at Key West'. The poet hears a woman singing as she walks by the sea. Is her sad song an expression of the 'dark voice of the sea', an echo of the 'ever-hooded, tragic-gestured sea'? Is it really the sea singing? No. The poem answers in its own particular way. The 'grinding water and the gasping wind' may indeed 'stir in all her phrases'. But the song is her own. She is 'the single artificer of the world/in which she sang.' She has the 'maker's rage to order words of the sea' and not only of the sea but also 'of ourselves and of our origins'. There is a need for order in all of us. For the sake of order we renounce simply echoing the vivid ebb and flow of experience.

Wallace Stevens set down one of the principles for his own poetry: It must be abstract. By 'abstract', however, he did not mean abandoning the vivid world of concrete experience and crossing over into a realm of pure ideas like the concept of a rectangle or the concept of justice. To abstract was to rearrange

51

the contents of concrete experience in a new perspective; a perspective lent by distance, perhaps, or by seeing things from an unfamiliar angle. In this process, the ordinary patterns in which the eye sees things is lost; but a deeper order in reality may be uncovered. An example might be air travel, a new and thrilling experience for the 1920s and 1930s. The air-traveller loses the sharp particularity of things, the small bumps in the landscape, the lanes, the hedges, the ditches. But a larger order appears, the whole line of a mountain-range, the curve of a coast, the jagged mass of a city. It is a new perspective. It is a bird's-eye view.

Abstract painters, though they may not go up in aeroplanes, work in a similar fashion. Abstracting is not leeching away the colour and immediacy of the concrete world. Rather it is re-arranging the facts of experience in a different pattern; not so that chaos may be concocted, but so that a different kind of order in experience may appear. Map-makers, at least the older ones, did something similar. They were not trying to picture a landscape. They aimed to draw a plan which would enable travellers to find their way from one place to another. Yet they did not cross over entirely into a world of conventional signs. When they drew in hills, the contours thickened into a resemblance to slopes. The heavy line of a road has a purposefulness, a directionality to it.

It is possible to make a quantum leap into another kind of abstraction. Think, for example, of why a wheel is round. The first clue is that all the spokes of the wheel are of the same length. Wherever you put your tape-measure, the distance between the rim and the hub is the same. It is already an 'abstracted' view and contains the solution to the problem. Yet 'spokes' and 'hub' and 'rim' are concrete words. We are still picturing the wheel in our minds. We can step outside this magic circle by saying; all points on the circumference are equidistant from the centre. A point has no size. A circumference is not a rim. A set of concepts have been introduced in place of pictures. A different kind of abstraction has occurred and a different level of universality has been achieved. The talk is of circles now, rather than of wheels.

'It must be abstract.' Wallace Stevens' words serve well to introduce the language of doctrine. The word has a number of meanings. It is often used to mean simply the teaching of the Church generally. However, the meaning intended in the title 'A Catechism of Christian Doctrine' is more precise. It envisages expressions of faith which represent a fair degree of abstraction, 'formulas of faith'. In the language of doctrine concepts and logic rather than images or symbols are dominant. This is achieved by a certain distancing (a 'bird's-eye view') from the vivid immediacy of our faith-experience; and a measure of detachment. There are, we have seen, different kinds and levels of abstraction and these are found also in the doctrinal language of faith.

Explaining and defending

Faith goes beyond understanding. It is something different from an ideology or a philosophy of life or a way of seeing the world. Yet faith 'seeks for understanding' by a natural impulse. We wonder, are curious, wish – to some degree even need – to know. We speak of our faith to others, we explain it, defend it. So it is necessary to express faith in a way which stands on the plain of common understanding. St Paul realised this when he stood in the Areopagus, ready to 'debate with anyone who would face him' when he contemplated the Epicurean and Stoic philosophers on the fringe of the crowd. It would not be enough to rely on Moses and the prophets, to evoke the perennial hope of Israel. He must not seem a 'propagandist for some outlandish gods'. Some new tack was needed. He speaks of the unknown God, the unique creator, the universal spirit unlike any human artefacts.

As the number of believers increased, opposition to them grew; a chorus of criticism and objection was raised. Some of this was composed of crude slanders. Christians were atheists, they practised incest, they were cannibals. The whole thing was a detestable superstition. This sensationalism could only be denied and allowed to die down. But some serious thinkers – Celsus and Porphyry for instance – raised objections of a different kind. How can a changeless God become man? Do not the gospels contradict each other? Why did not Jesus die a wise man's death, like Socrates? Some of these questions reached the heart of the faith and deserved serious answers. The apologists who undertook this task were speaking not to the household of the faith but to the powerful and the intelligent of the world. They had to concern themselves with making a case, with concepts and logic. They had to speak the language of intelligent public opinion, of Graeco-Roman culture. Through this a new way of expressing faith emerged; one which could stand up in the market-place of the world with arguments which had logical force.

Conflict and clarification

Apologists explain the faith to others. Theologians explain it to themselves and to their fellow Christians. Theology may stem from a natural curiosity, but often it arises from, and progresses through conflict. Early disagreements among Christians were usually over practical matters, though often a deep question of principle lay below the surface; how shall we deal with Gentile converts, must we extend the Jewish law to them? But the intellectual puzzles inherent in central Christian beliefs soon surfaced to be argued over with conviction and passion. So Arius contended that 'The Word is not truly God. But, if he is called God, nevertheless he is not truly so; but by participation of grace.'[2] Others found this quite at odds with their faith. God has truly become human, has taken a share in our nature, they said. Only thus is the world redeemed. Arius was anxious to preserve the unity and changelessness of God, his opponents to defend the divinity of Christ. Out of the dispute emerged a profession of faith with a new vocabulary; the words 'person', 'nature' and 'substance' stood for subtle concepts through which conflicting views might be reconciled. Here is a profession of faith whose tone and timbre is very different from the simple message of salvation; reflective, a little detached, logically muscular.

Athens and Jerusalem

The terms 'Athens' and 'Jerusalem' were not invented but borrowed from Greek philosophy. The concepts they expressed came to occupy a prominent position in the Christian creeds; giving them a philosophical tone, quite different from the accent of the Scriptures. This made some people uneasy. They feared the Greeks even when they came with gifts; indeed especially in that case. Were they turning 'the way' into a philosophy like Stoicism? Would Athens supersede Jerusalem? There was a certain crisis of identity here. Much earlier, the first believers had to decide how far they could shake free of Judaism and become a universal faith. Was it a question now of preventing that faith from being swamped by the immensely powerful Graeco-Roman culture?

What to make of the Greeks and their gifts? It was a question which went beyond using their concepts for the sake of clarity. It spread to a debate on how Christian initiation and formation should be conducted. Should it stay true to the initiation into mysteries, untainted by the old and elegant humanity of Greece? Or could a humane education be combined with catechesis? Many thought not. Tertullian said crustily that Athens had nothing to do with Jerusalem, was the adversary, the seducer. But those who favoured despoiling the Greeks won the day. A student at Origen's school wrote enthusiastically: 'Nothing was forbidden us, nothing hidden from us, nothing inaccessible to us. We were to learn all manner of doctrine – barbarian or Greek, mystical or political, divine or human. We went into and examined with entire freedom all sorts of ideas, in order to satisfy ourselves and enjoy to the full these goods of the mind. When an ancient thought was true it belonged to us and was at our disposition with all its marvellous possibilities of delightful contemplation'.[3] More succinctly and eloquently, Cyril of Alexandria wrote that there is one river of truth. Two streams flow into it from this side and from that; the stream of humane learning and the Word of God, 'the loveliest thing there is'.

Despite these enthusiastic accolades there remained some unease, some suspicion that the Greek roots in our profession of faith had grown more vigorously than the Hebrew ones. Since the doctrinal language of faith is most marked by this philosophical character, it was viewed in a cautious, sometimes dismissive way, not only in the age of the Reformation but, to some degree, in our own day. And, indeed, doctrine sometimes over-reaches itself, makes for itself exaggerated claims.

What doctrine is not

Doctrine is not a description of what is the case, like the formulas of chemistry or the laws of physics. Because doctrines are often cast in the form of propositions, X=Y, they may look like that. It is this similarity which misleads some people into thinking that doctrine is the real hard stuff of religions on which we build the other elements as we put marzipan and icing on a cake. But this resemblance is one of form rather than substance. Our doctrines are doctrines of the faith. It is out of faith that they grow and against faith that they are measured. They are not, therefore, like the formulas of science, the product of a process of observation, hypothesis, verification and conclusion.

Doctrines are not the object of faith; they do not give an exhaustive, or even an adequate account of that object. The true object of faith is its mysteries. We first of all 'proclaim the mystery of faith'; only secondarily do we give it rational expression. For these mysteries are not puzzles or enigmas which will be solved in the last chapter, or arrived at by the end of the tour. These mysteries are realities which by their nature cannot be clearly and completely grasped by the human mind. Doctrines have a real but secondary function in relation to these realities. They serve, medieval scholars used to say, as *'ministra objecti'*; they serve or mediate the reality, but they do not constitute it. 'The object of faith is not what can be expressed, but the reality itself.'

If doctrines are elevated into objects of faith, they may easily become idols. They may block our road to the realities of faith rather than opening it up. If moral rules are mistaken for the whole of morality, they may thwart their own purpose; as the Pharisees in the gospel made an idol of the law. Children learning to read sometimes develop a 'verbal façade'. They learn to use words without grasping meanings and so progress is thwarted. Similarly, there can grow up a 'doctrinal façade': a surface knowledge of propositions which blocks the road to the realities of faith, obstructing the pilgrimage of truth.

What doctrine is

Doctrine speaks faith cognitively, expresses it as a form of knowledge. It concerns itself with the clarity of concepts, with the strength of logical arguments, with intellectual coherence, with assessing the force of evidence. No doubt even the most dry-as-dust doctrinal formulas make some appeal to piety and prayer. But the main concern of doctrine is with clear and distinct ideas. We ought not only to feel compunction but to know its definition as well. We ought to be able to defend our faith in the intellectual market-place of the world. We ought to be able to explain it with clarity and force, in a way that is intellectually honest.

Development

Doctrine develops over time because, in this world, no formulations are ever final; because, 'here below, to live is to change and to be perfect is to have changed often'.[4]

Christianity is a historical faith. It professes that God's word has plunged into history; that we are not to extract ourselves from time and culture to arrive at some disembodied state. The Christian idea has an inner energy which drives it towards new formulations, more imaginative expressions, clearer and more compelling formulas. Moreover – like St Paul in Athens – the Church strives to attune itself to changing currents of human thought: to its mentality, its approach to logic and proof, evidence and truth. Events which occur, the discoveries of science, the achievements of technology, pitch new questions at Christian understanding. Old arguments appear in new settings, old formulas are called into question.

Newman's essay on the development of doctrine remains a classic source. For him an idea must develop 'in order to remain the same'. Otherwise it is washed up by the tide of time on some remote beach, a historical curiosity. For an idea, as the Christian faith is an idea, is a living thing. It is not a single simple concept like the idea of a centipede, but rather a 'great enunciation, whether true or false, about human nature or present good, or government, or duty, or religion ... carried forward in the public throng of men which ... is not merely received passively in this or that form into many minds but it becomes an active principle within them.'[5] As an active principle, it will be argued about, questioned and contradicted. New facets of it will be discovered, old formulations realigned; it will change direction sometimes and find itself in new intellectual territory.

In the course of its development, the doctrinal form of faith sometimes takes wrong turnings, goes down false trails. 'Christ is not truly God but rather a god-like figure'. 'Christ is not really man though He has taken on the appearance of humanity.' What happens when these crossroads are reached and the way ahead is uncertain? First, the Catholic tradition is that there is a self-correcting faculty in the community of the faithful. Faith has a sense, a nose for truth, an instinct for lines of thought which lead in the wrong direction. 'The people unfailingly adheres to this faith, penetrates it more deeply with right judgement and applies it more fully in daily life.'[6] This nose for truth is a collective gift, working independently of the teaching authority of the Church or the sifting of theological experts. Church authority represents, we may say, a second line of defence. Catholic belief is that there is a teaching authority in the Church and that, in important matters, it does not fail. It is invested in the bishops of the Church in communion with the Pope. This 'indefectibility' is not a miraculous gift which overrides fallible humanity. It rests upon knowledge and pastoral wisdom, upon fair-mindedness, understanding and far-sightedness. In the last analysis it guarantees that God, in his own way, preserves the 'magisterium' from going wrong when crucial issues arise.

To say that doctrine develops is not to say that it is relative; that it contains only a provisional and temporary truth. As we have seen, doctrines can be wrong. But what when the mistake is corrected and they stand foursquare in the line of tradition? They can be reformulated, certainly, as new evidence emerges, new circumstances arise, new ways of study are discovered. They remain true statements, albeit, as is later seen, limited ones. They stand in a line of tradition which is not handing on something inert like a baton in a relay. Tradition is a living thing which, because it has life, grows. When it stops growing, it is dead.

Dogmas of faith

In the course of history, some doctrinal statements have acquired special prestige, even solemnity. The creeds which we profess in the liturgy have a special resonance as truths of faith. The defined dogmas of Pope and Council make inescapable demands on us. We are to assent to these with – as Newman put it – a real assent; not as conclusions of which we are certain, but as expressing realities to which our hearts relate, of which we stand in awe. Must this mean that these dogmas are finished products, that in them the process of development has finally ended? That we profess their truth is beyond question. But how the Church understands them may change in the course of time. The great dogmas block off certain lines of thought. Like warning signs, they alert us to the hazards which lie ahead of travellers down certain paths. Yet they have also a positive aspect; they express for us the mysteries of faith. In this respect, they, like any human form of words, are not exhaustive, not final. They present, as St Paul said, a dark glass, not a face-to-face vision.

The hierarchy of truths

To reflect on the dogmas of faith is to realise that the geography of the world of doctrine is neither simple nor flat. It has its heights and hollows, its mazes, its points of vantage, its inner order. This order is often described as a 'hierarchy of truths', an important notion but one to be approached with a little care; for no truth is truer than another truth. Yet in the intellectual ordering of Christian faith, some truths clearly occupy a more important or central place than others. This is both because they lie close to what the Church sees to be the heart of God's revelations in Christ; and because they are focal points which unify other truths into coherent patterns. The doctrine of the Incarnation occupies a wholly different position in the Christian economy from say, the nature of the Sacrament of Confirmation. Not only does the whole faith stand or fall by it, but it also, in a tentacular way, gathers many other truths (about the value of fleshly life, about the Church) into the fold of meaning.

Any exposition of Catholic faith (such as the Catechism) must honour this order, this hierarchy of truths. But how can it be reflected in words, on pages? Some have looked to extrinsic criteria; the number of words, the number of column inches might tell us where each truth stands. But this is clearly not adequate. For a central truth might be expressed in a few words. A secondary one, more complex because derivative, might take a great deal of explanation. Equally, to apply theological notes – 'of divine faith', 'proximate to heresy' – is to make only an external classification. These notes are a useful, shorthand way of indicating the depth to which the teaching Church is committed to a doctrinal statement, but the inner force, the unifying power of a crucial truth of faith does not appear and much is lost.

The hierarchy of truths best appears when doctrine is presented in an organic way. The truths of faith are living and life-giving things, hold together, depend on each other. It is within this perspective that the order, the hierarchy, the logical geography of the truths of faith appears.

Real and notional knowledge

The power of story as an expression of faith is its ability to draw our feelings along the criss-crossing paths of event and character. We participate, we identify. Story can channel the feelings and rouse the imagination; and so it may hope to shape attitudes and lead to action. 'Life is for action', wrote Newman, '... the imagination has the means, which the pure intellect has not, of stimulating those powers of the mind from which action proceeds.'[7] Some stories may lead to action in a trivial sense; as an affecting tale may lead to tears. But others have a deeper, wide-ranging effect, those which are rooted in the roughness of the concrete, yet open to a larger perspective, 'not this or that particular man but mankind'.

Compared with the vitality and colour of story, the doctrinal language of faith seems, at first blush, pallid and pedestrian. Surely in speaking faith it is immensely preferable to use a language which catches the eye and speaks to the heart. Surely it must be more effective to do that, for 'logic makes but a sorry rhetoric with the multitude; first shoot round corners and you may not despair of converting by a syllogism'.[8] Would it not also be, in some sense, truer? In expressing facts, the stripped and clinical idiom serves best. But in striving to express mysteries, it is the oblique, the allusive, the complex, the spider's web of character, event and image which is most likely to hit the target.

Yet Catholic tradition makes much of doctrine. Its substantial dependence on Greek philosophy gives it an air of exactness and abstraction. Orthodoxy – the holding of approved doctrinal statements – is a requirement for Church membership. The value and importance of doctrine may appear more clearly in the light of Newman's distinction between real and notional knowledge.

Real knowledge then remains close to facts, to the concrete, to experience. From this closeness to the soil it draws its vigour and force. Notional knowledge is that of inference and conclusion; coolly distanced, clinically detached from the hurly-burly of our human condition. The same knowledge may be held in either way depending on the circumstances of the knower. The phrase 'the rule of law' means one thing to the student who comes across it in a text-book of social philosophy; quite another to a person who lives under the rule of apartheid or is oppressed in a South American dictatorship. The one has a notional, the other a real understanding.

In the perspective of this distinction, the language of story tends towards real knowledge. For 'the heart is commonly reached, not through the reason but through the imagination, by means of direct impressions, by the testimony of facts and events, by history, by description'.[9] Doctrines may sometimes lead to knowledge; their cool concepts transformed into realities so that a person may 'die upon a dogma'. But the general tenor of the doctrinal language is notional. The doctrine of the Trinity, so subtly formulated, so carefully chiselled, bears the mark, at least at first hearing, of an academic construction. What is the value – outside of academic – of the doctrinal expression of faith?

A clue may be found in another remark of Newman. Real assents 'sometimes called beliefs, convictions, certitudes ... are as rare as they are powerful... They create, as the case may be, heroes and saints, great leaders, statesmen, preachers and reformers, the pioneers of discovery in science, visionaries, fanatics, knight-errants, demagogues and adventurers'.[10] What these strange bedfellows have in common is that they are men and women of action. They are not people who coolly agree that something is the case. Rather they are driven by an idea, compelled by it. Real assent is St Paul impelled by his gospel to travel the length and breadth of the Middle East. It is also Don Quixote, as that lean and foolish knight, also in the grip of his idea, wandered through the great plain of La Mancha. It is exhilarating to be in the grip of an idea. But it is not always beneficial, not always wise, sometimes very destructive. Few assents have been more real than the Zieg Heils of the party rallies in Nuremberg. The language of notional assent, the idiom of analysis of evidence and proof, of premises and conclusions seems, by contrast, a drab and pedestrian path. Yet it is necessary to sift and substantiate the heady language of real assent; to discriminate between reality and illusion. Doctrine, because it stands back a little from the immediacies of faith, plays a crucial part in its development; in that of the individual believer and, even more, in the common faith of the Church.

Real knowledge, moreover, has about it a deeply personal character. It is rooted in experience, and the experience of one person is not that of another. Someone, we say, really believes in God. The reality of that belief rarely, if ever, depends on the strength of the arguments which support it. It arises rather from some moment of insight. Perhaps the person has been confronted by an inexplicable instance of self-sacrificing love, like the Machiavellian prince in Henry James' *Golden Bowl*. Perhaps some personal crisis has led to the perception that good and evil are more than categories of the social order. While such factors could hardly, in themselves, be called 'reasons', they are part of a reasoning process. For real knowledge grows only from the rich loam of experience. But they are obstinately personal. Such real knowledge is hard to communicate unless the experience which grounds it can be shared. Real knowledge, real assent then 'thwarts rather than promotes the intercourse of man with man'.

Stories, as we have seen, can carry real knowledge because they are constructed of event and character, of image and experience. But stories do not possess the instrument for sifting the true from the false. We must look elsewhere for that.

It is the business of notional knowledge to 'establish a common measure between mind and mind'. Notional knowledge is constructed of reason and logic, of premises and proof, of discourse and dialogue. So it is open to the world, is public property, can be shared and scrutinised. This communicability makes the doctrinal language especially important for the 'we believe' of the Church; for the development of understanding and the study of theology; for the solution of complex problems which require analysis and exactness. Newman remarks of notional and real knowledge that 'the latter is the conservative principle of knowledge and the former the principle of its advancement'.[11] With real knowledge we have a depth of understanding but tend to entrench ourselves in our own certainties, narrow but saved'. With notional knowledge we are open to criticism and dialogue, ready to reflect and to learn. These are virtues in faith and the purpose of the doctrinal language, distanced and flexible, is to realise them.

Lastly, the doctrinal language is, paradoxically, the language of tolerance. Conflicts erupt most fiercely when disagreements rumble below the surface. When they have been set upon the public table of reason and argument, they become, at least in principle, soluble. Bigotry is the occupational disease of real assents untempered by reason. To speak faith in the measured prose of doctrine sifts, complements and balances the compelling poetry of the gospel.

Standpoints and systems
Only rarely do doctrinal discussions take place in an atmosphere

of clinical detachment, reaching pure conceptual conclusions to be kept in a cool, dry, germ-free place. Theologians are affected by the burning questions of the day. They may represent, even embody, important ethical, cultural and religious values. Some are concerned with the position of women in history and in society and are committed to altering this. As theologians, it is not that they are going to step out of their role and argue the case rhetorically. Rather it is something always in their minds as they go about their work; an extra dimension to each of the problems they encounter. Others are most conscious of race as a factor in human history, one which they see appearing in all the spheres of life, appearing with especial prominence as they strive to formulate Catholic tradition in a systematic way. In this way feminist theology and black theology appear as recognisable 'schools of thought'. They are not systems in the sense of being self-contained and deduced from first principles. They are rather standpoints which colour a body of theology in a characteristic and distinctive way. Two important strands in theology today may illustrate and, let us hope, illuminate this point.

Theology of Creation

Few questions of the day are more burning than those connected with ecology. There is a world-wide, late-dawning awareness that we do not care for the world very well. We blunder about in it, and, being a high-tech generation, we blunder to great effect. Balances are upset, species destroyed, climates changed, the rhythms of nature altered with unpredictable effects. Linked to this is a vastly increased awareness of the life of the whole human race. Through the media and through easy travel, the lot of peoples once infinitely distant has become close to us and is starkly vivid. The world, sometimes called a 'global village', has become smaller, our common interests and destiny clearer and more compelling.

Theologians and all thoughtful Christians are affected by

these crucial questions. How shall they respond in their understanding and communication of Christian tradition? One reaction is to think that the formulation of Christian truth has become too other-worldly. The hope of salvation and the coming of the Kingdom of God have perhaps come to be interpreted in terms of heaven after this life and the reconstruction of the human world as a religious realm. Have Christians become too detached from human affairs, in spite of occasional forays towards social justice? Have they seen the tides, tragedies and triumphs in human affairs as important only in so far as they affect our other-worldly destiny?

So the conviction that our stewardship of the world, our responsibility for the planet is a value and a virtue in its own right, has been re-awakened. The command to Adam to name the animals, look after the earth, make it fruitful, has reappeared in a new and imperative light. The Second Vatican Council, moreover, declared the Church's solidarity with the people 'of our time'. The world is the 'theatre of human history, bearing the marks of its travail, its triumphs and failures, the world which in the Christian vision has been created and is sustained by the love of its maker'. It is a vision in which the cosmos and its inhabitants have their own intrinsic worth, a worth founded in the sustaining love of their Creator. It is a theological emphasis rather eclipsed in recent Catholic tradition, which has seen the world of redemption and grace as a small but brilliant circle of light, sharply demarcated, shutting out everything else into indiscriminate darkness.

To seek for the survival of God's creative love in the world is a different theological standpoint. It is not only that unspoilt nature continues to be 'charged with the grandeur of God' while human life remains under the ban of sin. The ascent of humankind too, with all its paradoxes, bears the mark of God's creative grace. The mastery of the world, the gradual humanising of it, contains on the one hand the danger of hubris, the temptation to build a tower which asserts and celebrates human self-sufficiency. On the other hand it moves towards the unfolding of human potential, towards, though falteringly, an order which respects the human person, towards the celebration of life in the arts. In the religions of the world too, even in primitive ones, lurks some remnant of an ancient wisdom; and beyond that, a quest for the transcendent mystery which stands in the heart of existence. For those who begin from this viewpoint, all these things stem from God's act of creation and are, in *some* sense, works of grace.

Yet across this path, like a dark ambush, falls the ominous shadow of the doctrine of original sin. This asserts that because of that first sin human beings are damaged in their natural lives and deprived, 'despoiled' of the supernatural relationship of grace. The large problems here are beyond the scope of this book. But let us glance briefly at the outlines of the argument. The 'damage to natural life' is not an insuperable difficulty. Anyone who looks at human history or at our present world will acknowledge that it is full of failures and setbacks; that is stumbles ahead; that it is marked by malice as well as good will. Yet the misery of our failures need not rule out the fact that our history is a limping progress towards the light.

To be 'despoiled of grace' is a different matter. It seems to empty human goodness and human striving of any substantial worth. In consigning it to the 'merely natural' realm, the impetus of God's creative grace seems ruled out. Yet many, in recent years, have been uneasy that the line between grace and nature should be drawn so uncompromisingly sharp. The distinction was made to defend the principle that God's grace is unmerited and freely given. With that purpose it was conceived of as separate from and stretched above our human, conscious existence. Yet the fact that God's grace is freely given does not mean that it is rare; as though if God were cavalier with grace he would devalue its currency.

Many argue that wherever spiritual and moral life is to be found it is 'within God's will for our salvation' and therefore graced even though not standing within the geography of Christ's redemptive mission. Should the graciousness and love which flows from God's creative act be seen like shards and shells, the debris surviving after a devastating cyclone? Creation theology answers No, it is densely present in the world.

Finally, what of the work of Christ? Is that not moored tightly to the dock of original sin? Did not God become man to remedy that great disaster whose crater lies across the beginning of our history? 'It was through one man that sin entered the world', St Paul wrote, and 'through the obedience of one man that many will be made righteous'.[12] Yet St Paul also writes of the mission of Christ in a very different vein. God's plan is that 'all in heaven and on earth might be brought into a unity in Christ'.[13] It is a vision of the cosmic Christ. The Word through whom all things were made is the Word through whom all things are redeemed. Creation and Incarnation are spoken in the same breath; two phases of the single act in which God who is love gives himself up for others. Creation theology takes its stand on this vision of the Word of God present (sometimes obscurely, sometimes unrecognised) throughout the universe.

Liberation theology

Liberation theology takes what seems, on the surface, the opposite standpoint. It surveys faith from the point of view of the destructive and dehumanising forces which are also densely present in the world, the forces of oppression. Many human beings, many of our brothers and sisters in Christ, live in crushing poverty. The necessities of a civilised life, the 'goods of the mind', even the requirements for an expansion of the spirit, are inaccessible to them. This comes about because of the way in which the institutions of the world are organised. Commercial interests, the forces of the market, the powers of capital and profit, hold them in an inescapable trap. Following the method of *The Church in the Modern World*, liberation theology begins with a descriptive analysis of this grim situation. The results of this analysis are presented as questions to Catholic tradition. What answers will emerge? How are these things to be understood in faith? How should we react to them as Christians in the light of the gospel?

Social analysis conveys a whiff of Marxism, and Marxist methods are sometimes used to lay open the workings of the world. But the response of Christianity does not speak of dialectical materialism or economic determinism. Rather what emerges is the deep biblical theme of liberation, most vividly expressed in the story and tradition of the Exodus. This theme – God saves us from slavery, from exile, from hostile forces – has, it is argued, become excessively spiritualised. It has become liberation from individual sin. But evil in the world, of which sin is the moral centre, is far more extensive. It is to be found in the institutions which condemn people to live in subhuman conditions, as well as in the hearts of those who initiate or connive in such structures.

From this standpoint the central teaching about Christ also has a different emphasis. It focuses not on metaphysical questions – person and nature – but rather on the preaching and action of Jesus in the gospel. His preaching of God's Kingdom reveals that God's will for human life turns on their head the values commonly held in the world, today as yesterday: success, prosperity, respectability, elegance. Blessed are the poor, the humble, the merciful, the persecuted. It is the marginalised who receive the blessings of God's Kingdom. Similarly, the Church is seen not primarily in terms of its defined essence; that is assumed. It is seen rather in its relationship to the world, to the quality, fullness and misery of human life. The Church is to witness to and promote God's values wherever it finds itself. Committed to his Kingdom, it is called to an 'option for the poor'.

Finally, liberation theology gives a high place to action in its ways of working and understanding. In its view, thought stands close to action and the two interact. So it is not a detached theology, not a study mainly located in the library or the lecture-room. Its idea of 'praxis' means action in the world to lift oppression. Yet it is also a theological method. For action has successes and failures and these give rise to fresh questions. The hope is that there will be a rising spiral of understanding. Marx said that philosophers had spent too much energy in trying to understand the world. The point is to change it. But the idea that we learn by doing is by no means a Marxist idea. Newman seems as far from Marx as you could imagine, yet here he is writing, 'Life is for action. If we insist on proofs for everything we shall never come to action: to act you must assume and that assumption is faith.' The point is not that faith is an arbitrary leap in the dark. The point is that action is a way of discovery as well as a way of changing things; from the standpoint of liberation theology, a singularly important one.

Holiness and truth

If doctrinal expression gains a stranglehold on faith there results a kind of religious rationalism. As we have seen, in the conflict of Athens versus Jerusalem, the former often represents a sceptical spirit which may encourage the spirit of dissent. Locke's evidential principle: 'do not entertain any proposition with greater assurance than the proofs it is built on will warrant' is, in itself, a narrow, lopsided account of reason and how it works. It is certainly not the way in which doctrinal understanding grows.

Newman remarks in relation to this question: 'In the schools of the world the ways towards truths are considered high roads open to all men, however disposed, at all times. Truth is to be approached without homage.'[14] *'However disposed'*: the dispositions here are more than intellectual sharpness, more even than a desire to be honest. For truth is not an open high road but rather a 'huge hill cragged and steep'. Pilgrims who seek the summit must go beyond intellectual honesty and possess a love of truth. They must go beyond that again and learn humility before it, so that 'errors, rationalisations, ideologies fall and shatter to leave one open to things as they are'.[15] They must have the courage of heart to pay the price of truth and abide by the consequences, wherever these may lead. The search for truth includes a moral and spiritual pilgrimage. For 'true learning begins in wonder, goes on in humility and ends in gratitude'.[16]

Chapter 3

FEELING AND FORM
The Language of Liturgy

The title of this chapter is that of a valuable book by Suzanne Langer. This is her argument. Reasoning and feeling are generally thought of, if not as contradictions, at least as incompatible ideas. Reasoning is 'cold' but reliable. Feeling is warm and agreeable but untrustworthy. Reason enables us to understand the world and to organise our lives. Feeling is an undertow below the surface of thought and action which may or may not be agreeable but which seems purposeless. Hence we should rely on reason – it is a safe guide to action and the arbiter of truth. We should be wary of feeling. It may ('wishful thinking') cloud our judgements; or it may ('being tender-minded') deflect us from firm decision. The reason for this is that reason is a reality which has firm checks and structures. It is confined by a chain of concepts and logical arguments which can be tested. Feeling, however, is formless flow. There is no way of checking its accuracy as a response to events.

Yet perhaps there are structures of feeling. These are not of a precise, objective kind like concepts and logic. If those were dominant then feeling would evaporate into rational thought. All the same, emotion, as a tendency in the human mind, does recognise happenings and does, in some way, judge them. Often it recognises danger and prompts swift action in response. The most notable example of a structure of feeling is to be found in the arts. Emotion is not a shapeless mass. It has an internal pattern, though this is not always recognised and formulated. Sound and semblance, shape and shade, word, image and assonance are moulded into a significant form. It is not a type of rational discourse. It is a form of feeling.

In this chapter, I shall try to apply some of these ideas to the liturgy as a language of faith. For, as a distinctive idiom, a mode of expression, liturgy shows some strong similarities with the arts. Sound, silence, movement, colour, duration – these are some of the strands out of which the web of liturgy is woven. Before turning to this, however, let us look at the geography of the liturgy; at some of the elements which constitute and shape liturgical life.

'Let us proclaim the mystery'

This call, loudly uttered in the heart of the Eucharist, acknowledges that the liturgy of the Church is not only its formal dutiful worship of God. It is that certainly; that 'faithfulness to the breaking of bread and the prayers' which we find in the Acts of the Apostles. It would be a mistake to envisage the liturgy as primarily a vivid and colourful way of expressing faith, still less a programme for teaching it. None the less it 'proclaims the mystery'; and the solemnity of the call implies that it does so in a way which is at least as effective as the narrative of the gospel or the formulations of the Creed.

This aspect of the liturgy appears vividly in the Rite of Christian Initiation. The catechumenate saw as its object the 'awe-inspiring mysteries'. Its purpose was the gradual initiation of candidates into these mysteries. Its programme contained a number of different strands. The candidate shared in the liturgy of the word but was excluded from the Eucharist; was integrated gradually into the community of faith and was subjected by that community to a number of 'scrutinies' – examinations of progress. The candidate was instructed and preached at, but the rites themselves played the greatest part. Ultimately the candidate entered upon the solemn Rite of Baptism; was questioned and anointed; must shed sin symbolically and make the decisive turn from West to East, from darkness to the light; was immersed in the water, received the white garment and the candles symbolising the light of truth. It was believed that the rite itself expressed the awe-inspiring mysteries both more adequately and more powerfully than any other language. What is it about the liturgy which is the source of this power?

A 'multi-media' language

The language of doctrine is the language of logic; that of story is woven of event, character and imagination. The weave of liturgy is richer still and more complex; it is composed of the threads of word and silence, of music, gesture and stillness, of sign and symbol, of colour and music, of stone, wood, space and time. Possibly, among the art forms, opera is the best analogy. Here, character and incident, aria and recitative, costume, movement and *mise-en-scène* come together and, in a good opera, are fused. The power of the liturgy stems partly from its multifoliate construction. How does this work? What happens to us when we participate in the liturgy? It is this question which concerns us here. Newman remarked, in discussing religious assent, 'I am not proposing to set forth the arguments which issue in the belief of these doctrines, but to investigate what it is to believe in them, what the mind does, what it contemplates when it makes an act of faith.'[1] In a similar way I ask what the mind does, what it contemplates, how the sensibility is affected, when we participate in liturgical rites.

Sign and symbol

These words occupy a central place in our understanding of the liturgy. A sign, says St Augustine, 'brings to the mind something other than itself'. Taken that way, the world of signs is a large and diverse one; from the natural signs of a change in the weather, to road signs and to the important conventional sign-system of language. Natural signs can be perceived by animals, as a dog will sniff out and bristle at the threat of natural catastrophes. Conventional signs belong in the human world of agreement and common understanding. Their place in the liturgy – especially that of language – needs to be discussed. But first let us speak of symbol.

Humankind, Ernest Cassirer thought, is a symbol-making creature. Sometimes we may speak of symbol as though it were a sign which has gone rather fuzzy round the edges; rather as metaphor is sometimes spoken of as 'simile with the "like" left out'. But a true symbol is something different from and much more than a sign. Think of the logos adopted by firms to identify and stand for their work. These may be very simple signs – the Rock of Gibraltar identifying an insurance company and standing for dependability and strength. But other logos are not drawn from the natural order at all. They attempt to express, in a much more oblique way, qualities in a company which are not easily, certainly not briefly expressible, but which make for reliability or for success. These qualities are, in a limited sense, 'mysterious'; and the designs which express them are, again in a limited sense, symbols.

A symbol does not bring to mind another known reality as the torch of learning on the roadside brings to mind a school. A symbol expresses a reality which transcends consciousness, which cannot be reduced to natural facts or concepts, which can be known only partially by the conscious mind. Some think – as Jung did – that symbols are a product of the unconscious. For them, the unconscious is not primitive – though it is 'archaic' – not composed simply of blind drives. It is also a collective psyche, even a collective wisdom which is not the achievement of individuals but which belongs to humankind as a whole. Hence these are certain symbols – water, for instance, and fire – which are to be found in all known cultures.

'Let us proclaim the mystery of faith.' It is not hard to see how these mysteries, known but not wholly conceivable, living and life-giving yet constantly going beyond us, find, most adequately, a symbolic expression. Some universal symbols spring from the unconscious of our race. They are gathered into the liturgy because some aspects of our faith are transformations of archaic human experience. But symbolic expressions (see the 'logos') can also come into being. So, in the scriptures and in the early Church community, symbols were found where stories and doctrines both fell short of being the expression of those mysteries which faith needed to express.

Marking time

Symbols, like music and colour, are positive forms, created or discovered to bear a heavy weight of meaning. Time or duration is a more elusive element in the liturgy, yet a very significant one. We are called to enter into the 'today of the living God' or into the 'hour of Jesus'; and it is possible to misread these phrases and imagine that the liturgy takes place outside time. Is it an eternal event without historical reference points? No, it is ordinary human time which is gathered into the weave of the liturgy. It is the procession of our days, the revolving cycle of months and years, the pattern of high days and holy days, the single arc of the seasons of our life. In the liturgy, writ small or writ large, human time is given a different pace and patterns. There are rhythms in life, say the heartbeat, which are rarely perceived or heard. The movement and pressure of external events is more strident and blocks them out. But sometimes they surface. We hear a different rhythm; perhaps we march to a different drummer for a while. In proclaiming the mystery of faith, the liturgy also proclaims the redemption of time. In the second part of this chapter, I shall look at these ideas in a little detail.

Liturgical language

Though there may be sermons in stones, human preachers use words as their medium. In upbringing and education, the development of competent and lively language remains a central concern. Those few feral children who have been found, brought up among animals and never exposed to speech, seem unable to make any real human progress. The advice, 'a single picture is worth a thousand words' often merely commends superficial sensation and a quick fix. It is through language that we learn to think, to relate, even to feel; language, William Walsh writes 'transforms the biological individual into the rational and historic person'.[2] Similarly liturgical language contributes largely to the formation of a person of faith.

So it is not surprising that the quality of liturgical language is a matter of great concern to believers; nor that any proposal to change it arouses strong feelings. In the Anglican communion, the introduction of new liturgical texts and the abandonment of old and hallowed ones is always worth a letter to *The Times*. In the Roman Catholic Church, even more acute problems have arisen, even more passions been aroused as the ancient Latin liturgy has been translated into modern languages, which have such a wide variety of structure and spirit. The bone of contention is often, on the surface, aesthetic – and this is not a minor matter. The old texts, the Book of Common Prayer, the dense, compact yet graceful Roman Missal, have great beauty, are works of some genius. The sonority of their cadences, the 'decency and sobriety of speech', drawn, as Peter Levi wrote 'from the teeth and the tongues of the dead and the anonymous'[3] conveys a sense of rootedness and perennial validity.

Opposition to modernisation, however, often goes deeper than this. Some think that to alter the language of liturgy is to change its very being; for that language, hallowed, consecrated by time, is a specially privileged instrument, a kind of incarnation of God's truth. To call this view 'archaism' is nothing to do with

'out-of-datedness'. It is a view of language as symbol. It sets aside
the dimensions of language that we call connotation and
denotation – the explicit communication of meaning. The
language in its exact self, its cadence and tone, its quantities and
music, conveys the meaning of the liturgy uniquely.

Archaism is an attractive viewpoint but it has a number of
weaknesses. One is that the dimension of explicit meaning
cannot be ruled out without damaging language at its heart. In
every language and especially in modern times, the meaning and
associations of words are forever changing. Old words become
beached in history and lose contact with the ebb and flow of
current usage. Or they lose their ancient force and acquire a
different tone and feel. Persevered with, an ancient text often
becomes something quite different from what it originally was.
Moreover, ancient texts do not lend themselves to the fusion of
tradition and contemporary experience which the liturgy sets out
to achieve. For these reasons, many churches have set out on the
road to translating or modernising their liturgical language; not,
for the most part, out of an itch to be different, but rather
'changing in order to remain the same'. Translation and
modernisation bristle with similar difficulties and the road which
has been taken is littered with failures.

Modernisation sometimes leads to a language which is slangy
and careless. This rarely has the power to draw our deep feelings
as liturgy should draw them. In the case of translations, there are
frequently done by committees – producing, it is sometimes said,
'mid-Atlantic English'. The purpose of the committee is to ensure
accuracy. To bring together a number of minds will guard against
personal bias, against idiosyncrasy, against flights of fancy. It is a
worthy hope. However, the aim of accuracy presupposes an idea
of equivalence between two different sets of words, either in the
same language or in different languages: and this ideal of
equivalence is far from simple.

Equivalence

To say that if an English translation sounds like the Latin original, it means the same, sounds naive. Yet it is surprising how influential such an idea continues to be. A translation should imitate, even mimic the original; not only echoing the words but following the word order, the syntax and the imagery. It seems to rest upon Locke's idea that there are concepts in the mind of which written and spoken words are the equivalent signs.[4] Men being able (like parrots) to make audible sounds should 'be able to use these sounds as signs of internal conceptions; and to make them stand as marks for ideas within his own mind, whereby they might be made known to others'. If the ideas are merely marks standing for internal conceptions, then if the marks are similar, the ideas will be similar also and will be accurately communicated. Clearly this is an over-simple, a mistaken account of the relation between thought and language and of the way language works. Translations which rest upon it, inevitably blunder badly

An old Latin prayer begins with the phrase:

Actiones notias quaesumus Domine, aspirando praeveni…

for which one old translation offers:

Prevent we beseech Thee Lord, our actions by thy inspiration

Where this translation goes wrong is in sticking close to the look and sound of the original words when the meaning of those which mimic them has changed, sometimes drastically. The word 'prevent', for example, has completely slipped from its Latin moorings. From 'go ahead of' with the positive sense of 'clear the way for', it has altered its predominate force to 'get in the way of and stop'. A dead language pickles its meanings like a fly in amber. But a living language changes, now quickly, now slowly, of its own momentum or in response to new needs, to social and technical changes, to events and circumstances.

An alternative version of the text runs:

Lord may your grace prompt our actions.

This departs from similarity of look and sound. But the word 'prompt' does gather up some strands of meaning – speed, intervention, correction, enablement – which 'prevent' has lost. Although it is not a similar word on the surface, it is a better equivalent. Resonances, flavours and atmosphere cling round words and are often lost in their derivatives. It may be possible to transliterate exactly the instructions on an electric kettle, but a prayer or a poem or a political speech is a different matter. For here there comes into play the hardly analysable web of stylistic devices, rhythms, balances, resonances and tone which we call the genius of a language.

Good translation requires an imaginative leap; and this not for the sake of elegance or style, but for the sake of equivalence. The fact that liturgical texts use moral and doctrinal teaching, or more often, rest on it, applies another level of discipline. The liturgical translator must pay attention not only to the original text in itself but also to its cultural and theological context. Given that this is accepted, an imaginative translation will always be a closer one.

How does the liturgy work?

'To investigate what the mind does, what it contemplates when it makes an act of faith' was Newman's question. We have considered something of the geography of liturgy as a language of faith – its many-sided character, its use of symbol and language, its relation to time. What happens within human beings when by free choice they become part of this weave? A clue which leads in the right direction is this. In considering doctrinal assent we ask what the mind does. In speaking of liturgy we often find we are speaking of feelings. They are altered, redirected, shaped, drawn. Although this distinction between mind and feelings is over-simple, it sets us on the right road. The question of the relation between feeling and the liturgy as a language of faith is the one to which I now turn.

Feeling and form*

The life of feeling has been much scrutinised by philosophers. Their accounts undermine our simple reports – 'I am anxious', 'I feel sad' – with analyses of great variety. The passions of the soul known immediately and invulnerably through introspection? Mental states known only by behaviour and learnt through belonging to a language community? In medicine, too, the emotions are a matter of concern. 'Psychosomatic', a word taken with increasing seriousness, bears witness to this. For some the emotions are a reservoir of primitive energy, bubbling blindly into consciousness, channelled only with difficulty by the structures of personal and social life. Others see the emotions as a vapour of the mind, given off by the activity of nerves and muscles. Drugs, not talk, can reach them and set them in order. Yet others think that at the heart of the emotions lie the deepest patterns of human meaning. They are in touch with consciousness of the race.

Artists deal with the emotions unselfconsciously; not holding them at arm's length but using them as the stock-in-trade of life and work. The romantic thought that a poet should be like an Aeolian harp, set in a tree, tuned to resound when the great winds of feeling blow. The business of the artist, Suzanne Langer argues, is to make out of semblance, air or image, a significant form which is an analogue of emotional life. In the mirror of art we

---

* The substance of this section appeared in *The Contours of Religious Education*, ed. J. Astley and D. Day (Mayhew-McCrimmon), and is used here by kind permission of the editors.

recognise our inner selves. The rough particularity of image or story is so set in a form as to speak of and to 'not this or that particular man but mankind'.

Emotion plays an important part in religious life, though religious believers – especially theologians – are not always ready to admit this fact. Feelings – often caricatured as 'enthusiasm' – feature largely in the pathology of religion but cut a poor figure in the cool orthodoxy of conventional belief and practice. Shakers, Barkers, Holy Rollers and Hot Gospellers are made to seem the archetypes of religious emotion. The exuberance of their religious practice – heartfelt no doubt, yet anarchic – seems a poor guide to the complex world of doctrine and practice. 'What must I believe?' 'How must I act?' The sweeping away of these questions in a tide of feeling subverted religious order and menaced its social respectability. Yet precisely in undermining the subtle structures of religious tradition, the revivalist meeting created a nostalgia for the simple and the passionate which came to seem a more authentic mode of faith; a certain envy for those who

> sang their Amens
> fiercely, narrow but saved
> in a way that men are not now[5]

The Protestant Reformation, Nietzsche wrote, was a revolt of the simple against the complex. In the Catholic world, a couple of generations ago, reason and will were definitive, doctrine and law their instruments. Emotion was suspect – product of raw force, concupiscence, which it was the business of mind and will to subdue. In the seminary the arts were discouraged unless they could be disciplined into safe forms such as church music. They were banished for the same reason which led Plato to drive away the poets – although crowned with laurel – from the ideal republic. Their incarnations of power must come from the regions where the dark gods dwell. They could have no place in the city of God, would threaten its battlemented doctrine, undermine its serried laws. There were, of course, popular devotions of a dramatically emotional kind. But these were conceded rather as the Grand Inquisitor gave bread to those from whose shoulders he had lifted the burdens of thought and freedom. There were, of course, Catholics who took the arts more seriously. But even they shared the prevailing opinion that the function of the arts was a decorative, not a substantive one; as Sydney argued that the honeyed words of poetry served to make palatable the bitter rhubarb of morality. Enthusiasm for the arts, or trust, as Keats put it, in the truth of the imagination, was viewed as the early Cistercians saw the Cluniacs. It exuded a faint but unmistakable aura of corruption. It was an uncomfortable reminder of the courts of Renaissance popes and Josephist emperors.

Over the last twenty years emotion in religion has regained respectability, indeed has exploded into Church worship, into pastoral relationships and into spiritual counselling. No doubt this reflects some deeper change in our mental climate. Leonardo Boff, in his book on St Francis, suggests that we stand at the end of an age. This he calls the age of *logos* in which the instrumental – analytic reason – was king. It was the concept that counted. Symbol and mystery were eclipsed. The purpose of knowledge was power. We stand at the beginning of a new era, that of *eros* and *pathos,* of affection and sympathy. It is the heart, Boff argues, which determines the premises of all possible knowledge for 'the ultimate structure of life is feeling'; not only because this is the way the human psyche works but also because it is the way in which human nature is constructed. Words that move in such a cosmic sweep cannot easily be brought to ground by close analysis or argument. For myself I sense a deep truth in them: as one recognises in the weather forecaster's prediction what the farmer sniffs and the sailor feels in their bones.

The rehabilitation of feeling is not without its problems. Its results are not always happy ones. *Eros* looks to *logos* for its regulation. Loose feeling without forms or targets is indeed a demonic force. Plato and the Church were right to be nervous about it. It is often said of bad poems that 'the plangency is all on the surface'. It isn't embodied in the muscles and sinews of imagery and form. So in Christian worship and other aspects of the life of faith, an enthusiasm for spontaneity and openness sometimes releases a lot of emotion which is raw and formless; and this is usually hard to handle and sometimes downright dangerous.

Like many others in the aftermath of the Second Vatican Council, I had high hopes that the liturgy of the Church would be the summit and the fountain of renewal. These hopes have not altogether been realised and I suspect that one reason may be that the relation between structure and feeling in the liturgy is not well understood. Suzanne Langer speaks of music as 'a tonal analogue of emotional life'. I would like to see what can be made of the notion of the liturgy as a structure of feeling.

Some might object that this way of approaching the liturgy is too analytic. It murders to dissect. Rather than speaking of thought and feeling, better speak of 'experience' as an indivisible fact. 'Experience', like 'need' – another popular word in discussions such as this – is an ambiguous word, sometimes a mischievous one. It is often a way of avoiding questions, especially epistemological questions, by presenting a self-authenticating *fait accompli*. Its protean being is often contrasted with the 'bookish' or the 'academic', greatly to the discredit of the latter. The academic shuts himself up in an airless library stuffing his head with Shakespeare or Wittgenstein until his veins silt up and he gets weevils in his brain. The devotee of experience lives in the fresh air and knows what's what along the pulses and in the guts.

Although I am a little wary of arguments to which the concept of experience is central, I recognise that there are more subtle understandings of the word. Henry James writes of it as 'an immense sensibility, a kind of huge spider-web of the finest silken threads suspended in the chamber of consciousness and catching every airborne particle in its tissue. It is the very atmosphere of the mind'. The relation of feeling and form in the compounding and the vitality of that atmosphere is precisely what I intend to discuss here. *Eros* depends on *logos* for its regulation, *logos* on *eros* for its life. Neither thought nor feeling is absolute monarch. Each fulfils its proper function in relation to the other.

In this discussion, I have three questions in the forefront of my mind. The first is: In liturgical worship, what is it to mean what we say? The second: What is the relation of feeling to liturgical words and acts? The third: How, if at all, is feeling altered through participation in liturgical rites? Although I do not treat these questions systematically, they provide focal points for the whole discussion and a summary of its conclusions.

Let us begin with a funeral. Funerals are said to ritualise grief and present the clearest case in which liturgy is recognised to be psychologically beneficial as well as religiously important. Grief, pain, lostness, and the way in which we deal with these feelings, lie at the heart of the liturgy of death. Recently a custom has grown up which, far from ritualising grief, ignores it to concentrate on other matters. White vestments are worn, cheerful hymns are sung, the liturgy is centred on the Resurrection of Christ. This seems to me a mistake, a tendency to allow liturgical renewal to be overwhelmed by theological principles or even fashions; so that its main lines of force derive from religious ideas rather than from the existential reality of faith in the world. Newman complained of the philosopher Locke that he 'consults his own ideas of how the mind should act instead of interrogating human nature as an existing thing as it is found in the world'. Of course there must be a dialogue between doctrine and liturgy. But we ought to beware of the imperialism of the concept.

Such didacticism has been a particular danger for Roman

Catholics since the introduction of the celebration of liturgy in the vernacular. The transition from a dead language to a living one opened up new areas of liturgical communication. It was easy in the early days to slip into identifying this new form of communication with notional understanding. The meaning of words must be clear, the significance of symbols made plain, metaphors transposed into ideas. In some extreme cases there occurred a gross distortion of the very nature of liturgy; its transformation into a didactic lesson. There is certainly a time and place for the exposition of Christian beliefs about death, judgment and eternal life. A funeral is not such a time, nor such a place. The way in which the rites embody these beliefs is enough.

Ritualising grief involves three things. Firstly, it makes a private grief a public fact, since the liturgy is celebrated by the whole community. Secondly, it sets it in a tradition; liturgy carries the Church's tradition – not a baton in a relay, but a living, organic growth – steadily and more powerfully than any other idiom. Thirdly, it places grief in a different context of meaning, not through didactic expressions or 'words of comfort', but by drawing grief into the more powerful net of symbol and sacrament. And so grief is altered. It is drawn into a new place where it has not lost its sharp edge but has changed its bearings. When we look at it in this way, 'ritualising' throws some light on the question 'In liturgy, what is it to mean what we say?' Private feeling finds a public context. All of us are saddened and sobered by death. The liturgy expresses our common feeling in a faith-filled way. The private grief of the bereaved differs from this common feeling. It is personal and raw. Yet it is connected with the common fund and is drawn into it.

Often we feel hypocritical when we proclaim ourselves filled with joy at the memory of Christ's resurrection or the conviction of our redemption; when in fact we are feeling liverish, worried about money or irritated with the bishop. Such discordant feelings do not invalidate common worship. It is enough to be there, to participate, to enter into the ritual words and acts. The faithful feelings which motivate us to do that establish us in the common reservoir of felt faith belonging to the Church, and our ruffled emotions are reset in a different context and so altered. This is one reason behind the Vatican Council's requirement of intelligent participation in the liturgy. It is from liturgical worship that the faithful 'derive the true Christian spirit' and this requires that 'their minds be attuned to their voices'. The sense of 'mind' here is not the abstract intellect but the sentient being, *eros* as well as *logos*.

We can speak then of feelings being redirected through liturgical acts and so altered in themselves; rather as a different context can change the meaning of an event and so alter the way in which it is experienced or even perceived. The uniformed figure glimpsed through the glass door ceases to inspire nervous anxiety when it is recognised that he is here to read the meter. So, by setting feelings in a new context of meaning, by drawing them into a common fund of meaning, liturgical rites are able to alter their bearings. This may become clearer if we consider the connection between feelings and external events or states. Changes in such events or their disappearance or even their reinterpretation can alter feelings in several ways, causing them to evaporate, lessening them, even reversing them. Sometimes this is because the external event which changes is the cause of the feeling. I discover that the buff envelope with a window contains not a tax demand but the butcher's receipt. But the objects of emotions and their causes are not always the same. We might say, 'I was irritated with the children because it was my fiftieth birthday'. Here the children are the unfortunate object but the cause is the sadness of ageing. Rather vague, ill-defined emotions are often focused on an object which is not their cause. Sometimes – as in the above example – this connection is irrational and disordered. But not always. My fear of death may project itself to salt or saturated fats and here there is a real connection.

The word often used for the object of emotion is 'target'. Sometimes the wrong target is found, simply by some kind of emotional mistake. 'I was angry with my wife so I kicked the dog'. But sometimes the targets are really connected with their cause; and this may be reasonable and beneficial. One function of liturgical acts is to provide targets for feelings which are connected with their cause. The grief of the bereaved is caused by the loss of someone loved. The rites are also about that event. They provide a secondary target for grief but one which is really connected with it; setting it in a context of common faith and, in this different perspective, changing its bearings. It is also, I shall argue later, a function of liturgy to move feelings from targets which are genuinely mistaken, to those which are true and appropriate.

We sometimes use language which suggests that feeling is a kind of perception – 'I feel the truth of your remark.' But clearly this is loose talk, for feelings do not give us new information about the real world. On the other hand, feelings most often entail some belief. If I am fearful at meeting a lion it is because I hold certain beliefs about the habits of lions. These are probably correct but the beliefs entailed in my fear of mice or spiders or heights are probably mistaken. Yet as we all know, it is sometimes not possible to alter people's feelings by showing that the beliefs involved in them are mistaken. A neurosis is such a feeling, attached to an irrational target, and not to be dislodged by concepts or logic.

The emotions central to the life of faith are also sometimes based on mistaken beliefs. We may be in awe of the wrong things, such as statues or the music of Tallis or Church authorities. We may feel guilty about the wrong things, say the accidental breaking of rules. The power of these mistaken beliefs is not to be broken by reading the Catechism or by a good talking-to or even by the study of theology. For these remedies deal only with the notional assents which have no power to move us. Notional assents lead to repose rather than action or struggle; which is why, writes Newman, intellectuals who deal in them are rarely devout. Liturgy, however, has the power to lead our feelings towards different targets.

I have suggested that emotions are sometimes diffused from their cause to other targets which have a real connection with it. Such transfers we call reasonable, or, better, appropriate. A liturgical act, say a sacrament or a funeral, does not have the same organic connection with death or forgiveness, that salt or unexploded bombs have with the prospect of death. It is an artificial or constructed target, more like the horrific warning signs we see near army firing ranges. The purpose of these is to translate our feelings into motives for action – we are to avoid this area. Liturgy sometimes does this. It may lead us to conversion, to a different way of life. But its first effect in serving as a target for our feelings is what I have described as giving them new bearings or a new context of meaning. Liturgy does this because of its mediating or transparent quality. It does not gather feelings to itself as to a final end. It works according to Aquinas' principle: the terminus of faith is not the expressible but the real. Sign, symbol, music and gesture make present, in a uniquely powerful way, the mysteries of faith. In this, liturgy is similar to the arts, which do not focus our feelings finally on an object, but lead them through it to a participation in experience or the recognition of our own. So the Christian funeral does not ritualise grief as the Lord Mayor's show ritualises his status. It actualises a Christian tradition of faith and feeling into which personal grief is gathered.

I have spoken of liturgy as an 'idiom of faith'. The adage *'lex orandi, lex credendi'* (law of prayer, law of believing) implies the same principle of finding two modes of expression; though the prayerful one is clearly very different from that which is composed of concepts and logic. In describing it as an idiom, I do not mean that liturgy has all the characteristics of a language.

It combines, rather like opera, several different media and each strand retains its own characteristic mode of working: music, verse, gesture, symbol, etc. Still, liturgy has its own distinctive principles, through which the several strands are subsumed into a new whole.

To characterise liturgy as a mode of expression, we can make use of Suzanne Langer's distinction between discursive and presentational forms. The discursive form is propositional. It moves through a series of logically linked stages from a premise or problem to a conclusion or solution. Each stage in this movement is indispensable, but only until its logical force is established. Once that is done it can disappear into oblivion, for attention is focused only on the correctness of the solution or the conclusion. So, discursive thought never impresses us as a whole, nor can it do so, for in its movement through time, only the conclusive moment is significant.

Presentational forms on the other hand do not move in the same way through logical space, dismissing each stage when it has served its purpose. They are compounded not of concepts and logical links but of semblance, space, symbol and metaphor. The elements are linked in such a way that their interrelatedness in one glance is what constitutes significant form, what makes the form expressive and communicative. This is true even in the case of music, where duration in time, the disappearance and reappearance of themes, is of the essence. For musical time is not chronological time. The form is not present to us until the last note is played.

Liturgy is the presentational form of faith. Its presentational characteristic makes it an effective target for feeling, though an unsuitable one for analytic thought. It is characterised – as D. H. Lawrence wrote of the novel – by 'subtle interrelatedness' rather than logical structure. Lawrence went on: 'communication can only happen when a whole novel communicates itself to me. The Bible – but *all* the Bible – Homer and Shakespeare are the supreme old novels. These are all things to all men. Which means that in their wholeness they affect the whole man, which is the man himself, beyond any part of him. They set the whole tree trembling with a new access of life, they do not just stimulate growth in one direction'.[6] Notice that the whole man alive includes intelligence – *eros* requires *logos* for its regulation. But the real source of life is the flow of the vital feelings, and the liturgy has the power to draw these away from things which are mistaken or dead towards things which have in them vitality and truth.

These high-flown ideas seem a long way from yesterday's Evensong or from next Sunday's Mass. Let me try to bring them some way to earth with another example. This is the Rite of Reconciliation. This sacrament is the most individual and private of all. Its substance has become, over the centuries, the totally secret and detailed acknowledgement of sins guarded by the seal of confession, with a cursory and rather legalistic absolution. It has thus become totally detached from liturgical tradition and connected rather with Church authority ('the power of the keys'), problems of conscience and spiritual direction.

Apart from the oddness of a sacrament being wrenched from its liturgical setting, there were other causes for unease in this situation. One was that the classification of sins (mortal and venial, kinds and categories) led to a rather external behaviouristic moral outlook and consequently attached guilt to the wrong targets. The renewal of this sacrament set out first of all to restore it to its place in the public worship of the Church. Sin is social as well as personal. It occurs in the Body of Christ. Reconciliation too should occur within the Church community and should be a public act. Also this sacrament is an object (target) for feelings of guilt.

Guilt, although it has had a bad press in the literature of religious psychology, is not in itself a morbid or unhealthy feeling. It is harmful when it is loose in the psyche or attached to irrational or mistaken targets. We feel guilty about our sins; quite rightly so. But, as I have suggested, guilt is often misdirected or short-circuited. Concentration on external acts and their classification leads guilt sometimes to focus on these and to disregard intention and the heart. We feel guilty because we have broken a moral rule, and the rule, the focus of our guilt, becomes a kind of idol, occupying the place which, in the Christian moral life, should belong to God alone. So there grows up a narrow, legalistic moral outlook which fails to break through into the truly religious sphere. The public liturgy of reconciliation – readings, prayers, music, gesture – sets out to lead the flow of our feelings away from a blinkered and legalistic morality into the Church's common fund of feeling; and beyond that into the mystery of God's reconciling love and the assurance of forgiveness.

Another way of describing this process is to say that the liturgy leads us to conversion. The word raises many hackles; the archetype is what occurs as a result of an evangelistic sermon which is often said to be 'too emotional' or even 'mere emotion'. I think what is implied here is that such a stimulus looses emotions – which may be fear, joy or even self-disgust – without providing targets clear enough or strong enough to channel their force. Edwin Muir in his *Autobiography* describes his two youthful conversions, to evangelical Christianity and to Marxism.[7] Both provided an immediate resolution of emotional tension, but neither lasted long. The liturgy deals with feelings in a gentler, more oblique way. Its subtle interrelatedness, its multi-faceted unity, its doctrinal and institutional strength, enables it to draw and contain feeling in a way which is more sure-footed and offers greater steadiness and permanence. Of course what the liturgy does is deep and complex and therefore gradual.

Bernard Lonergan writes of conversion that it 'is a change of direction, indeed a change for the better. One frees oneself from the inauthentic. One grows in authenticity. Harmful, dangerous, misleading satisfactions are dropped. Fears of discomfort, pain, privation have less power to deflect one from one's course. Values are apprehended where before they were overlooked. Scales of preference shift. Errors, rationalisations, ideologies fall and shatter to leave one open to things as they are and to man as he should be.'[8] Although Lonergan is interested primarily in a comprehensive theory of knowledge, his idea of conversion as invariant in structure though occurring at different levels, illuminates the argument here. Knowledge is certainly involved as 'errors, rationalisations, ideologies fall'. But values are also apprehended, preferences shift, one is liberated from fears, inauthentic life is unmasked. The invariant structure, yet the varieties of embodiment, offer an image of multi-faceted unity of the liturgy and of its power. The presentational form of Christian faith embodies that faith in many ways. Its 'immense spider-web' is subtle and powerful enough to bring the different levels of conversion together.

This sacrament is an example of how liturgy arises when particular events in our lives are touched by the mystery of grace; the beginning of life, marriage, ministry, the inner collapse of sinfulness, the *'tempi forti'*, times of power. There is another way in which the whole stretch of our lives and our feelings is drawn and directed by the liturgy. A first case of this is the annual liturgical cycle, in the course of which, it is often said, we live through the Paschal mystery. The word mystery – a truth of such range and scope that it lies beyond exhaustive expression – fits most naturally into liturgy of all the idioms of faith. The liturgy, as Paschal, is not an exposition of the doctrines of Incarnation, Redemption, Sanctification. As a presentational form, avoiding didacticism, liturgy is able to leave aside problems and concepts and has a power to express the mystery itself. Its meaning goes beyond following prayerfully the events of the Lord's historical life. Rather, we can say, it embodies the mystery of God's redeeming grace as this is enfleshed in the life, death and resurrection of Jesus. Its power lies in the 'subtle interrelatedness' of word, symbol and action which draws us into its movement. We identify; through following in the footsteps of Christ's earthly life, we are able to work our way into the reality which that life embodies, into the rhythms of Incarnate grace moving in history. When we watch *King Lear* we identify with character and action; we are attracted, appalled, saddened, puzzled. We also go beyond that, to enter into the truths and values which are there embodied: clash, fall, triumph. 'All truth is a species of Revelation.' In the liturgy, this identification is with the words, actions, failure and triumph of God's word made flesh, of which indeed, all human truth and value is a fragmentary reflection. So the flow of our vital feelings is drawn into the pattern, rhythms and meaning of death and resurrection. As a pedagogy, the task of liturgy is to people the world of imagination and feeling. This I think to be the deepest meaning of the Council's teaching that it is from the liturgy primarily that we derive 'the true Christian spirit'.

Each year is a year of grace. God's power, made flesh in Jesus, moves through it, drawing the ebb and flow of our deep feelings into its own redemptive pattern. In the liberal west, we have grown used to a life with a very low degree of patterning. This is because of our liberal and permissive ideals which lead us to minimise the structuring of life in order to allow the maximum elbow room for personal choice. In earlier folk societies, structures and demarcations were numerous and clear. The stages of life – birth, adolescence, adulthood, marriage – were clearly marked out; vital social functions such as war and fertility were also solemnised by ceremonies and rules. So, everyone knew where they stood even if, 'narrow but saved', no one saw very far. The danger of our way of life – the point has often been made – is the danger of meaninglessness, lostness, anomie. The blurred and crumbling concept of 'life-style' cannot bear the weight of our deep feelings. This is why we find that many people – especially the young – are drawn towards authoritarian total systems.

The liturgy is neither authoritarian nor total. It is a strong framework of meaning which encompasses the principal passages and stages of our life and how we move through them. So the beginning, establishment and active independence of life is the existential ground of the sacraments of initiation. Crucial areas of marriage and ministry are sacramentally solemnised. Human decline – failure, suffering, death – is encompassed by sacraments of wide pastoral range and scope. This is especially true in western Catholicism. Here – in opposition to the 'sudden life' initiatory sacraments in Eastern orthodoxy, and the 'adult ideal' of Baptists – sacramental life is marked by stages and gradualness. The sacramental principle encompasses a faith journey, marked, as life is, by different stages and levels. The sacramental pattern contains and engenders a strong sense of purpose but one which can be renewed and re-created at different levels and in diverse life-situations. Its meaning is not fully revealed until the arc of life is complete; as a symphony is not grasped until the last note is played.

Chapter 4

THE TRUTH IN LOVE
The Language of Morality

I – INTO THE MORAL MAZE

The proof of the pudding is in the eating. The proof of a faith is in its results, in the kind of life which flows from it. Actions speak louder than words, at least in the sense that when we encounter a life marked by generosity, compassion and courage we sit up and take notice. Arguments may be forceful and testimonies eloquent but in themselves their effect is limited and transitory; for fine words butter no parsnips. Of the early Christians it was said, 'see how they love one another'. The quality of their lives may not have been the most exact expression of their faith, but it was the most compelling. In the modern west there is a deep division between thought and action; truth and goodness are not obviously intertwined. But the Hebrew mind saw things differently. Knowledge was of the flesh as well as of the intellect. The word was not only a thought spoken but a deed done. So to St Paul the phrase 'doing truth' came naturally. In doing truth we not only authenticate beliefs but also come to discover their deeper meanings.

As a language of faith, story is part of a larger narrative genre which is universal in human culture. Doctrine adopts the accents of philosophy and liturgy belongs to the world of symbol and rite. Christian moral life equally is part of a larger life; that world of principles, rules and relationships, of rights and justice, ultimately of good and evil, which constitute our common life as distinctively human. While Christian morality has distinctive elements and its own particular quality and timbre, it must be seen in the general context of human moral life. Morality is not a sub-department of religion. It has its own ways of working as a language has its grammar and its syntax. In this chapter, I shall look first to map the world of morality, its landmarks, its logical geography. In the second part I shall discuss the one element which makes Christian morality distinctive.

The human person

Most moral systems base their principles in some way on the dignity of the human person; the rights and responsibilities which flow from that begin to weave the moral web. Christian faith takes up this position and reinforces it through the belief that each human being is an image of God. The Catechism of the Catholic Church briefly introduces its moral section ('The Faith Lived') by way of this truth. Human persons are created in Christ, 'image of the invisible God', to be themselves images of the Creator. This likeness is realised in the communion of persons. It implies the presence of a 'spiritual and immortal soul', the source of an ability to understand the order of the world and to take one's own destiny in hand. The image of God in us is damaged by sin so that moral life becomes 'a dramatic struggle'. None the less it subsists. Human beings are 'the only creatures on earth that God has willed for their own sake'. The human person alone constitutes a 'subject' and therefore may not be treated as a means to some other end. In this assertion of a right which may not be overruled, begins the perception of a moral order in the world.

The human subject as a source of morality should not be seen as a spiritual being, solitary and self-sufficient. We are embodied subjects and the body has its proper claims. Through the body we are linked to a larger world. Through speech and gesture relationships begin and so we are bound into a common life; one which goes beyond 'respecting rights' to become a world of love, sympathy, care, concern and compassion. Again, we are part of the human species, and the well-being of that species has a bearing on our choices, for instance in our sexuality. We are also part of a larger world still, our 'environment', living and inanimate, whose future has recently been seen to be so closely interwoven with our own. It is this human subject, many-sided like a prism, multi-dimensional, which is the source of our 'moral being'.

From this source emerge the 'human goods', those values which represent the fullness of humanity. About these there are many arguments, indeed some problems which will probably never be solved by pure reason. To clarify them we look to the gospel and to Christian tradition as well as to logic and the moral wisdom of humankind. These values – life itself and its continuance, justice, truthfulness, peace, compassion – form the framework of a moral order. They are sometimes spoken of as 'absolutes', though the word needs to be used with some care. For they are not like Plato's 'forms', an eternal form of a table, a concept of justice, timelessly and immutably existing in another world. Sometimes these values might be in conflict – for instance truthfulness and charity – so that a moral dilemma is created. A person may lay down her life in the interests of some other value; in some cases the life of another may be taken. Still these values begin to form a moral order in the world which is objective. It ensures that morality is not purely a matter of emotion ('how we feel drawn to act'), nor is it entirely a matter of motive and intention ('meaning well'). Both of these factors form important strands of the moral weave. But beyond them there is an objective moral order, there is the natural law.

Natural law
The word 'nature' names a slippery concept. In the eighteenth

century, when it was widely and confidently used, its very changeableness provided a key to the cultural and literary history of the age. In the neo-classical period it stood for what is universally perceived as orderly and uniform; 'true wit is Nature to advantage dressed, what oft was thought but ne'er so well expressed.' By the end of the century it had turned topsy-turvy in the landscapes of Capability Brown, the 'Gothick' novels, Thomson and eventually Wordsworth; 'natural' came to mean what is wild, disordered and particular. We should approach the word with care.

Behind most uses of the word 'natural' in moral discussion lurks the large and persistent presence of Aristotle. For him the concept of nature flows from the perception of right functioning. We know what a knife is for, we have seen it 'do its thing'. And so we know how it should be made and how it should be used; and also, how not. It should not be used for breaking open locks nor for removing recalcitrant screws. We can see the function of a drinking glass and know that it should not be used for keeping goldfish in.

Of course Aristotle knows that human beings are not knives or drinking glasses. But he thinks that a perceptive observer can know enough about human life to see how it should be when it is working properly. 'Right functioning' in human beings is a complex thing, best described as 'virtue'. But it can be seen when it is there. The judges at the Nuremberg trials acknowledge this possibility in their verdict on war criminals. Their judgment depends not on international law nor on any written code. They invoke 'crimes against humanity'. In doing this they acknowledge that there are limits beyond which human beings cannot be allowed to act, limits which stem from the very roots of human life itself, which are, in some way, 'natural'.

Christian moralists have been quick to seize upon this persistent ideal. Is it not fully in tune with St Paul's teaching that pagans who had never heard of the law can point on Judgment

Day to 'the substance of the law engraved on their hearts?' (Rm 2:15). Even without revelation, he argues, they have enough moral awareness to stand in the light of God's judgement. For this inner law is no arbitrary imposition. It stems from the nature of things, from the very heart of being. For 'the light of natural reason by which we discern what is good and what is evil … is nothing but the impression of the divine light upon us'.[1] Centuries later the Second Vatican Council sounds the same chord. 'Deep within his conscience man discovers a law which he has not laid on himself but which he must obey. For man has in his heart a law inscribed by God.'[2]

However, it is one thing to catch your pig, another to take it to market. The natural law, seemingly so rich in possibilities, proves remarkably difficult to cash out in the hard currency of concrete action. Not much can be learned from observing human behaviour as a sociologist or a psychologist might. Cultures are diverse, customs and laws various, normative patterns difficult to detect. Biology, apparently the most obvious field in which a well-functioning human being (like a well-functioning knife) might be studied, proves a dubious ally. Moral arguments which depend on it, for instance those concerning contraception, frequently get into a great tangle. Human purposes and biological ends are not always in perfect alignment. Biology does not define a human being as the cutting edge defines a knife. Moreover, natural law theory assumes a nature which is fixed and final. The modern (equally the post-modern) world, if it thinks of 'nature' at all, thinks of it as flexible; thinks of it as possibilities and projects for the future rather than as the fact which the past reveals. In this it is aided and abetted by the vast vistas which the progress of technology opens up. It is a society dramatically tilted towards the future.

The natural law is lodged more precariously in self-knowledge and, with greater frailty still, in the world community ('crimes against humanity'). In the Christian moral language of faith it is certainly important but to be handled with care. If we handle the Greeks and their gifts gratefully but with kid gloves, the same should be true of Romans and their laws.

Yet the adoption of natural law theory in Christian moral teaching has one huge advantage. This is that by invoking 'nature' as a moral source, by calling on something which, though elusive, is a universal element in human life, it plunges into the universal moral discourse of humankind, into that long, unended conversation. Christian moral teaching thus ceases to be peculiar to a minority, even a large one. Its teaching becomes universalisable; presenting duties, obligations and ideals which rest upon all. In doing this, natural law becomes an instrument through which the gospel can be preached.

Law and love

'Nature' is a slippery concept but 'law' appears an admirably clear one. Its clarity is what recommends it to moralists; none of the penumbras or ambiguities of relationships, ideals or virtues here; only the sharp outlines of certainty. Yet, for Christian moralists, law, while a most useful category, is also a highly dangerous one. Lawmakers work most often in the cause of justice. Yet above all they wish to avoid ambiguity. Justice 'seen to be done' is their most active concern; that it is in fact done, their assumption. Hence, though law may hope to establish the limits of say, murder with intent, its ineradicable tendency is to describe and classify outward, observable behaviour. To enter the inner world of intention and motive, is to plunge into murkiness. Yet intent and motive are never secondary factors but constitute defining characteristics of moral action: 'it is from within, from men's hearts', says the Lord in the gospel, 'that evil intentions emerge' (Mk 7:21).

To say that intent and motive should be considered first is not to deny that laws are important. If they have an inbuilt tendency to veer towards the external, motive and intent, relationship and feeling tend, conversely, towards the wholly subjective, towards a moral universe which is not only blurred but cannot easily be held in common. So laws – the natural law, divine law, the old law, the new law – affirm the presence of an objective moral order in the world; and, to a greater or lesser degree, they systematise it.

Legalism is the outlook, the cast of mind, in which law is the chief category and the main horizon of moral life. At its worst it can amount to a kind of idolatry; law comes to occupy in life the place which should belong to God alone. In less dramatic cases, legalism may constrict, even emasculate the spirit of the gospel. The spirit, so luminous, so vivid, so life-giving, we catch on the wing as it were, in the Beatitudes, the two great commandments, the parables, the Lord's priestly prayer. The attempt to reduce these to a code of laws is like squeezing an orange and filtering off the juice. All that remains is the rind and the pith. We have seen often in this book that formulations become desiccated unless they draw life from experience, unless there is a constant shuttling between the two. So with Christian moral teaching – if law is the vivid foreground of Christian life, its heart, as we shall see later in this chapter, is love.

Sin and virtue

Sin is an offence against God; an act contrary to his will, consciously and freely chosen. Such an act is among the first recorded in the history of salvation. Adam and Eve had laid upon them one prohibition, which they disobeyed. The second Adam reversed their disobedience through his Passion and Death, but its effects remain with us and in us. It is not surprising then, that sin should be prominent, sometimes overwhelmingly prominent in Christian moral thought. Life is a dramatic battle against sin. The two ways, towards happiness and towards perdition, lie open before us at every turn. We are frail and damaged creatures. We are surrounded by temptation. Only constant watchfulness, discipline and self-denial fortified by grace can preserve us from being lost. These themes create a style of moral teaching based on solemn and sombre truths. No one would deny that there exists in our human reality much weakness and some malice. Yet the way in which these truths are ordered, the consequences drawn from them, the resulting tone and timbre of this style raises some questions.

A moral landscape dominated by sin is like an island dominated by the towering presence of a volcano; the country coated with the ash of failed choices. When we speak of virtue the sky brightens. A new note is struck, one of growth, progress and purposefulness. Virtues can increase, they take hold of us, become part of us, make goodness flow naturally. Virtues are habits. 'Habit' is not a glamorous word. It has a mechanical ring. Often we dismiss virtues as 'mere habits'. Yet habits have their value. They are the defences we set up to surround our deep commitments; to preserve them from being eroded by the grind of daily living, by chance, by circumstance, by weariness. Those habits which we call virtues, also contain an element of power, empowerment; as when an official says, 'By virtue of the power invested in me, I...'; or when Chaucer says of the sweet showers of April, 'of which virtue engendered is the flower'.[3]

Virtues are often classified into the human and the supernatural; prudence, justice, fortitude and temperance on the one hand, faith, hope and charity on the other. The latter are said to be 'infused'. God gives them to us, though we have to work at preserving them and making them grow. Faith, hope and charity flow from the gospel, rather than from the old and elegant humanity of Greece. Yet all human virtue is God's work and in some sense is energised, obscurely or openly, by the presence of grace.

A moral life which hinges on virtue has a positive charge, a tonic atmosphere. It does not eclipse the elements of law and sin or make them superfluous. Prudence prevents us from playing fast and loose in moral matters; aware of our frailty, aware that these are situations and circumstances which may be beyond our power to cope with. Justice is a quality which gives to laws their validity. As a virtue it disposes us to respect and observe laws. Charity leads us to go beyond them. Almost inevitably, a moral teaching which ranges itself round law and sin faces us, like a Plimsoll line, with a minimum below which we must not fall. The path of virtue is not static but urges us onwards and upwards. So it acquires the character of a pilgrimage – for the Christian a pilgrimage of faith. Morality ceases to be a minimal baseline from which growth may perhaps begin. It becomes integrated into that larger spiritual quest in which we seek to become, inch by painful inch, the unique person that God wants each of us to be.

It is possible to keep laws with almost military precision. But virtues are neither exact nor codified. They are essentially embodied. They live not in rulebooks but in persons, not in the abstract but in history. We do not learn virtues as we learn rules, nor grow in them as we become more punctilious. It is in narratives, in stories, that we perceive them; as the Old Testament epics embodied the ideals of Judaism, as the lives of the saints set before us Christian holiness in all its variety. As we identify, enter into stories and feel our way through them, we are able to share, at first vicariously, but then in reality, in the qualities they represent; we grow in zeal with St Paul, in justice and courage with St Thomas More, in universal love with Mother Teresa. The phrase 'the following of Christ' is a lens which concentrates the pursuit and hope of virtue. It does not call us to slavish imitation. It calls us, rather, to enter into the Lord's life as we discover it in the gospels, and so to find the vision and the courage to embody the qualities of that life in our own, in ways to the outward eye vastly different, to the inward, organically the same.

Conscience and responsibility

'This conscience doth make cowards of us all.'[4] Under the surface of Shakespeare's image lurk several elements. Conscience is somehow debilitating. It saps manly decisiveness. It can lead to a paralysis of action. Hamlet was a man of the Renaissance. He had left behind the sturdy public morality of the Middle Ages, in which moral borders were clear and colours sharp. He is thrown back on his own inner resources. He thinks also of conscience as a faculty in him, or a drive which conflicts with other drives. It struggles against the desire for revenge. Will it win? Or will revenge win? This is the drama. In our own time also we adopt the language of conscience as a faculty, a moral 'sense' like the sense of hearing. We speak of 'examining the conscience' as though it were rather like consulting your watch or checking the weather forecast.

Yet there are important differences between conscience and our faculties or our drives, which do not have the essential connection with reason that conscience does. Conscience is based on self-consciousness, on reflection which leads to a rational choice. It is concerned with responsible decisions based on reasonable judgements. Yet conscience goes beyond reason. It involves not only general principles which we can think out and formulate with our minds. It also involves concrete decisions; and in the world of the concrete, the specific, the particular and the individual, feeling and imagination come into play. It is their province. There is a large gap between judgement and decision over terrain which requires not only that we keep a clear head but also that we mobilise the affections. Conscience is best thought of as an orientation or a dimension of the whole person. Conscience is myself, when I am aware that I am morally responsible; responsible and therefore accountable, to myself, to others and before God.

Conscience first

Conscience is sacred. It is, the Vatican Council says, 'man's most secret core and his sanctuary'. And Newman, in unusually unbuttoned mood writes, 'I will drink to the Pope, but to conscience first'. A convinced conscience is to be followed against all odds; against the loss of prosperity, of reputation, even of life itself. Equally it is to be held in respect, whether we think it right or whether we think it misguided. No one should ever be forced to act against conscience. However, when it comes to acting on conscientious convictions, other considerations sometimes arise. The interests, even the safety of others may be involved. No one would force a Jehovah's Witness to accept a blood transfusion, for that principle of conscience must be honoured in itself. But when it comes to preventing their children from receiving blood, many state governments deny Jehovah's Witnesses that right, considering that the life of a child outweighs in this case the right of conscience.

Informed or educated?

'Conscience must be informed and moral judgement enlightened' says the Catechism of the Catholic Church (1783). There is more to it than 'doing your own thing', though that is often praised as a sign of sturdy individuality. When push comes to shove, doing your own thing usually means being driven by whims and fancies. Similarly, the popular concept of 'life-style' proves on inspection to be rather thin and threadbare. It is as though the matter of how we live our lives were of a piece with having good taste in ties or a liking for package holidays. Conscience deals with the realities of right and wrong, of good and evil. It is thus radically different from personal preference or subjective liking.

On the other hand, the phrase 'an informed conscience' can also be misleading. For it suggests that there is a body of moral information which you can learn as you learn the Highway Code, in the light of which conscience will work properly. But moral knowledge, moral reasoning, even moral judgement, is only half the moral loaf; better than no bread perhaps, but the more inert half all the same. Beyond the acceptance of principles we need also the abilities which will get us across the deep gulf between judgements and practice. For example, we have to be able to foresee with some accuracy the probable consequences of our actions. If I choose to do this, then probably the interests of X will be affected in that way. If I turn a beggar away sharply, not only will the beggar go hungry but his children will probably do the same. We also have to learn how principles can be applied to practical cases. It is one thing to have a passion for justice. It is quite another to see how the principle of justice applies in some hotly debated question in local politics when there are good arguments on both sides. To do that requires more than a sharp mind. It is, Karl Rahner writes, 'the holy art of finding the concrete prescription for one's own decision in the personal call of God; in other words the logic of concrete particular decision which also does justice to eternal regulative principles.'[5]

'*The personal call of God*': the phrase serves as a solemn reminder that conscience does not work like a calculating machine. Its heart is a personal responsiveness. It lives and must thrive none the less, in the moral maze where difficulties and dilemmas are frequent. Acquiring the abilities – skills even – which make possible this 'holy art' is a matter not of information but of education.

Mother and teacher

This view of conscience ('Christ's vicar', 'sanctuary of the soul') can leave the impression that moral life is a rather solitary affair; lived by a lonely, autonomous individual wrestling with her own dilemmas in a kind of reverent vacuum. But in fact, conscience is rightly subject, and open to a number of influences from outside, both in its formation and in its present action. Jean Piaget's account of moral development sees it as evolving from concern with the material content of an action ('You make a big blot, it's a big sin') to an awareness of motive and intent (if you didn't mean it, it isn't wrong). He also sees it as beginning as a response to adult authority ('We have to do it, they said we must'); and evolving into a free decision made in the interest of social co-operation. It is a thesis which begs as many questions as it solves. Other writers in the same field have found it correct in its main lines but mistaken in so far as it envisages the commands and prohibitions of being outgrown, shed, buried in the anonymous past. Adult interventions play a positive role. They are interiorised and persist even though their form may change.

Freudian theory, too, is sometimes read as though the super ego were a purely negative force, an unconscious conscience lurking in the shadows of unreason to persecute us with small but continuous stabs of guilt. It also comes from outside, from adult prohibitions, from social pressures. Sometimes we imagine that if it could be depth-charged, made to surface and subjected to the cold light of reason and logic, our moral unease would dissolve. Such hopes are both impracticable and unprofitable. The interiorising of the adult world and the standards of society are necessary to moral growth. The unconscious conscience may sometimes run riot and cause havoc but it cannot be done without.

Authority then has, in one way or another, a positive role in moral growth, and in moral life also. Moral questions are common property as well as private choice. They are shared, discussed, debated among friends, between opponents, in the media, in parliament, in the Church. The Church possesses, indeed is, a tradition of moral wisdom – a tradition, of course, which lives and grows, not a code set in stone. It has grown up over centuries, through reflection on the gospel, through attention to the problems Christians face in the world and through the work of scholars and saints. Its contents are consequently a mixed bag: principles formulated from natural law and from the moral demands of the gospel; a body of case law which applies these to concrete human choices; ascetical and mystical teaching.

This tradition of moral wisdom exists first of all in the whole community of believers. As the faithful corporately have a sure sense of truth, so also they have an unfailing instinct for the right and for the good. Within the community there exists also the teaching authority, vested in the bishops in communion with the successor of Peter. It is to this mainly that the Catechism of the Catholic Church refers when it speaks of the Church as 'mother and teacher'. The two words are significantly different. A mother gives birth and nurtures. The Church regenerates her children as moral beings; enabling them, through word and sacrament, to speak their 'Yes' to God and to understand what that 'Yes' implies, in terms of their attitudes and choices. She gives birth in them to the taproot of morality and the foundations of holiness. The teacher can never stop short at announcing moral rules like a government department. To teach is also to listen to the experience of others, to perceive their strengths and difficulties, to lead them towards greater understanding and greater moral courage.

The long road

At one time, moral theology tried to be comprehensive; to envisage every possible situation in which a Christian might find himself and provide a ruling for it in terms of describable behaviour. How much can you steal before it becomes a mortal sin? The answer was there. Could it be right to give an untrue reply if good will come of it? Apply the principle of double effect and here comes the answer. This system in one way made moral life easier. There was a comprehensive code and no ambiguities. Yet it was a system which had some weaknesses. In focusing so thoroughly and so exclusively on external behaviour, it inevitably eclipsed motive and intent and shrouded the 'Yes' to God in which Christian morality finds its meaning. It was a system which could be made to work in a relatively simple world. But today technology and research are expanding the horizons of choice in a bewildering way. It is the age of freezing embryos, cloning and the prospect of environmental catastrophe, of the inner dynamics of the human mind and feelings also. It is a world 'difficult to understand'. To classify all the choices open to people today is beyond human possibility.

It is, writes Karl Rahner, a long road between general principles and concrete choices. At one time, Church authority could at least attempt to walk all the way down this road with the individual Christian. In a few matters it still does; saying for instance that the direct killing of the innocent is always and everywhere wrong. But in many areas of morality this proves impossible. The Church says, 'Here are the principles, from natural law, from the gospel. Here are some of the ways in which the principles can be clearly applied'. But there comes a crossroads, a point of separation. Beyond it the Christian is on her own. Her conscience, informed and responsible, is what will enable her to travel the rest of the road in faith.

So the moral maze grows more complex. However, the heart of Christian morality remains unchanged. This heart does not appear in the workings of subtle moral dilemmas. This heart, as the gospel makes clear, is to be found in the morality of love.

II – MORALITY AS LOVE
We are perhaps passing from the age of *logos* into that of *eros;* from an era dominated by the problem and the technique into one whose motif is sympathy and imagination. If love really characterises the *Zeitgeist,* if it is the theme of the age, can it really count as a feeling? Can it be listed along with fear, sadness and anger, among the emotions, those more familiar (if still mysterious) inner realities which so trouble us and yet generate in

us so much energy? Again, we use the word in so many different ways. I love Mozart. I love single malt. I love justice. I love you to distraction. To love God truly is to love your neighbour. How can Mozart, single malt, justice, a person and God possibly be targets for the same feeling?

Christians believe love to be the very being of God. 'God is love, and he who lives in love, lives in God and God lives in him.'[6] We believe God's inner life to be one of relationships; the Father speaking the Word and so generating his only-begotten Son; the love between them springing to personhood as the Holy Spirit. We believe also that the finite world is an outpouring of God's love which is in its essence creative. This was Dante's vision after he had run the gamut of human misery, squalor, falsity, malice and despair, in the circles of hell and purgatory; to come 'near to the limit where all wishes end' and to see the ultimate reality of God's love both unifying and energising; binding the scattered pages of human history into a single volume; and when vigour failed him finding his will

> roll'd onward like a wheel
> in even motion, by that love impelled
> that moves the sun in heaven and all the stars[7]

... *l'amor che muor'il sol e l'attre stelle*'. It is significant that what Dante feels to be driven by God's love is his will. It was a faculty of paramount importance to medieval theologians; to us, too, it is important, though problematic also.

The Four Loves

It is difficult to connect this transcendent force with our feelings for the trumpet-playing of Bix Beiderbecke or for the girl next door. We cannot deduce them from it nor explain them by it. What we can find is more of a family likeness. Our human feelings of love (when they are authentic, even if they seem trivial), are refractions in the situations of life, so diverse, multifoliate, of that life-giving force. Since the circumstances of our lives are so various, human love, like a chameleon, takes a thousand forms. The liturgy of the Church gathers private grief into the Church's common fund of feeling and so gives it different bearings and a truer meaning. In a similar way, the creative and unifying love of God gathers our human loves, so limited and faulty, into the mystery of his own, where both their true meaning and their distortions stand revealed. To make this connection, as Dante found, is a work not for the abstract mind but for the imagination; both a leap of the heart and an arduous journey of the spirit. C. S. Lewis begins his excellent *The Four Loves* with the remark that the structure of his book would be simple. He would simply treat of need-love and of gift-love in turn. But, he acknowledges, he quickly recognised the distinction to be over-simple and the direction which it took misleading. Indeed, as the advice goes, 'If I were going to Killarney, I wouldn't start from here at all'.

Christian ministry – service of others in the name of Christ – supported by the Church is, almost by definition, one of these refractions of God's love. Yet God's love became truly human. What we know of it, what we practise of it, we learn from (and are impelled by) the Lord's humanity. And this humanity was (and is) the same as our own. 'The one who sanctified and the ones who are sanctified are of the same stock.' Jesus, in his human life, went through the same processes of growth as we do; was subjected to the same stresses as we are; lived necessarily in his historical time and culture as we must. We cannot deduce from Dante's vision what the shape and form of ministry should be, as an expression of God's love. A perception of that transcendent love as the ultimate meaning ought to irradiate our understanding. But we must begin in more homely places.

Lewis was right to begin from the down-to-earth concept of need. But he soon discovered that the projected thesis that need is love's primitive beginning, gift its refined fulfilment, was one that quickly landed him in difficulty. For it is odd to be forced to say that the child who runs to his mother for comfort is showing a love which is of rather low quality, not quite the genuine article. Moreover, our love for God is necessarily, in the first place, need-love. Whatever gifts we give him – our substance, ourselves – cannot but be a response to this and in some way dependent on it.

Nevertheless the notion of need is, if not a good pivotal term for a large explanation, at least a good point of departure. 'Without a doubt', writes Hans Urs von Balthasar, 'nature brings the reality of love to us from our subhuman roots; for love is built into the foundations of living beings'.[8] We need to take the more humble routes, as Aquinas advised the seeker for truth: 'by the little rivers only, you will find your way to the sea'. Those who take more dramatic plunges sometimes find themselves in waters deeper than they can swim in. Leon Bloy once remarked that there are certain pious people who, because they never learned to love anyone, think they love God. The ideal of loving God, or the duty to love God, are sometimes used as an excuse for not venturing into other paths which, on the one hand, are more risky and demanding, but, on the other hand, are indispensable. Human love, with its attendant vulnerability, puzzlement and heartbreak, schools us for a world where love has more cosmic dimensions which we demarcate by the words 'exchange', 'covenant', 'dialogue', 'alliance', 'communication', 'need' and 'gift'.

Need is certainly a basic concept when we speak of our need for air, water and warmth. Some writers have given the word a much wider reach and speak of a 'hierarchy of needs'. These extend from the basic need for food, through the need for affection and relationship, to our final for 'self-actualisation'. A scheme like this is useful enough for a teacher who is trying to tap effective sources of motivation. Its weakness is the arbitrary use of the concept of need itself as an outside category within which all of these realities can be placed and identified. This in turn gives the impression that need is the sole force driving our learning and our behaviour. This is surely mistaken, for other aspects of our humanity emerge at various points and take on their own life. One of these points sees the birth of love. Need remains a force throughout life, but it is right to speak of 'need-love' in its own right as well as acknowledging the 'need for love' which we undoubtedly have as a subordinate member of a sequence.

A different route is taken by the philosopher Emmanuel Levinas.[9] For him need envisages as its object impersonal being and its activity to assimilate that being for its own survival or satisfaction, as an infant assimilates air or cries for food or warmth. The tiny child is imprisoned in the self. How is he to achieve the feat of moving outside it? One road along which he goes is that of enjoyment. To enjoy food, to snuggle easily in bed, to be amused by a funny face is to turn aside from the mode of assimilation, to perceive hazily that there is a reality beyond the self: 'earthly nourishment; the pleasures through which the self deceives its solitude'.[10] Another way is focused in the distinction between need and desire. The former simply assimilates. Desire wants, but perceives that it may not get. It perceives otherness, something strange and different from the self, which cannot be reduced within one's own thoughts and possessions, and which has its own rights. For Levinas, this perception of the other is the root from which all subsequent morality grows. It is immediate and primary. 'Morality is not a department of philosophy, but is, itself, the first philosophy.'[11] No problems for him about deducing an 'ought' from an 'is'. Embodied in the 'epiphany' of face and voice it leads to the perception of persons and their rights (not of course one which is in any way conceptualised).

'To see a face is to hear already the words, Thou shalt not kill.' This awakening of the self to the radically other is the birth of morality and the root of love. The face which smiles, the voice which is heard institute the world of exchange, of giving and of welcoming. Other philosophies, Levinas writes, make too much of knowing and having, of seizing and mastering. 'Knowledge has always been interpreted as assimilation.' This wish to assimilate the other remains a temptation. About erotic love, he has this to say: 'The idea of a love which is a confusion of two persons is a piece of false romanticism'.[12] Love should make the other more himself, not diminish his identity.

If this analysis contains some truth, it follows that there is something in Lewis' original perception of love from being need to being gift, though the two terms need to be used carefully.

Balthasar writes in a similar vein when he speaks of love as being the unique path of revelation. Cosmology – perceiving God in the natural order of the world, and anthropology – perceiving God through human qualities and possibilities have crumbled. Love remains – a perception of another who is not to be intellectually mastered or understood. What confronts us in love is a 'miracle'. It cannot be analysed for it cannot be other than it is. We are always 'surprised by joy'. It is like the startling epiphany of beauty. 'The finale of the Jupiter symphony ... can only be as it is ... unless perhaps, Mozart were alive to change it.'[13] Though St John speaks of Christ as *logos,* implying reason and philosophy, this *logos* proclaims himself 'love and grace (*charis*) and as such the Glory (the divinely beautiful, *doxa*) and thus precisely as the truth *(aletheia)'.*[14] Other approaches seek to assimilate and grasp. The third way of love recognises, acknowledges and responds.

If love is an epiphany of joy it is also an arduous journey of the spirit, beginning like Dante's in a dark wood with no clear way ahead; growing, perhaps, but always at risk from the frost of instinct and circumstance. The danger which most obviously threatens it is the urge to dominate; to use others, to exploit them to our emotional advantage, or to assimilate them into our own system. In the past, philosophers have sought to assimilate data within a single system, sometimes doing violence to the data of experience, distorting it to the image of themselves. In a humbler way, we often catch ourselves assimilating a new and disturbing idea into our existing outlook, reshaping it so as to blunt the sharp edges of its challenge. Philosophy is not meant to be only – perhaps not at all – a source of consolation.

It happens with people as with ideas. To perceive them as 'other' does not always open the way to gift, welcome, dialogue. The other may be seen as a threat; it stands on its own feet, the independent, the unassimilable. Parents rightly want to hand on to children the heritage of their culture and values, the harvest of their lives, of their love. Yet mothers are often possessive. They perceive their children as precious, yet with a love shot through by a sense of ownership. They tie them to their apron-strings, and it is well-known what profound harm frequently follows. Fathers, too, in fact as well as fiction, sometimes want sons cast in their own image. The boy must be called to the bar and drink claret, he must drink Bass and work at Ford's, he must go into the army, he must avoid such unserious trades as the arts or social work. He must be an extension of the father's personal system. Henpecked husbands serve their wives' need to maintain the world according to their own order. Wives who are battered physically or verbally threaten their husband's self-sufficiency. The risk of love being influenced – even absorbed – by assimilation or dominance, is greatest when there is, in the structure of a relationship, a strong element of power. Power is present potentially in families, actually in government and industry, and in the Church. For spiritual power is the most far-reaching of all, probing beyond outward behaviour into the citadels of mind and conscience. Hence it is the most dangerous kind of power, though also an indispensable one. For some must 'speak with authority' as Jesus did. Those who are called to that authority are, in the same breath, called to an eminent ministry of love.

Extremely delicate matters of conscience and belief are involved in both sides of this ministry. Pastors run the necessary risk of distorting their subjects' true shape by assimilating them piecemeal into their own system. Love enables people to grow along the lines of their true selves. It promotes variety rather than sameness and in this way achieves unity rather than uniformity.

Even counsellors, whose job is not to speak authoritatively but to enable others, experience the temptation to dominate. Counsellors are trained not to give answers or instructions. Their task rests on a more absolute recognition of the 'other'. They are to help clients to think for themselves, to recognise and cope with the nature and force of their feelings, and so to make their own decisions about their own lives. Yet who has not felt the frustration of watching others behave foolishly while we know quite certainly that we could tell them exactly what to do? Most of us are quite good at solving other people's problems.

If the other person is seen (probably unconsciously) as threatening, assimilation or domination is one way of defending the boundaries of the self. The best form of defence is attack. Perhaps so, but there is another common way, that of strategic withdrawal. Some people, more introverted, perhaps more sensitive, find themselves lured along this road. They refuse to play the game of relationships, refuse to risk their hearts with anyone. They retreat into small hobbies and little luxuries. This temptation also is well-known to those called to ministry. Their calling is to be always available to those in their care, and availability, though it sounds a very negative virtue, can characterise a very demanding life. We are involved in dramas which are dramatically painful. We listen to interminable stories so trivial as to seem a waste of time. It is no mean feat to recognise the other, to persevere in exchange and dialogue, to answer need with the gift of attention, continuously and faithfully. Those who are celibate are particularly vulnerable to this way of escape. Withdrawal is, for them, an easy rather than an irksome task, for they have no constant reminders of what they are doing. Children are not the only hostages to fortune. A call to ministry is one also, but one more easily evaded.

As well as counting among our deeper feelings, love also (some would say supremely) concerns the will. We find in the gospel the harsh and uncompromising saying: 'If a man come to me and hate not his father and mother and wife ... he cannot be my disciple'.[15] Again, 'If you love me, keep my commandments'. Texts such as these seem to discount sympathy and dialogue, alliance and gift as true forms of love. They seem to suggest that the love of God, in Christ, should lead us to outgrow, even jettison, the heart's other affections. They seem to deny the idea with which this chapter began; that human loves generously undertaken are embodiments of God's love in human affairs and also the little rivers by which the unfathomable sea is reached.

The theologians of the Middle Ages from whom we derive so many of the ideas through which our faith is expressed and systematised propound a similar teaching. An object may first impinge upon our 'sense appetite' and, being desirable, draw us towards it. But the desired thing passes into the intellect to be judged conducive or not to our ultimate good. Then it is for the will to choose it or deny it and it is in this act that love is principally to be found. Although, of course, the teaching of the great scholastics is much richer than this bald summary suggests, it does appear to locate love in a world of reason, order and weighed choice, which seems to us rather clinical and bloodless. In the catechisms through which many learn their faith the same impression is given; that love inhabits a world of cool and bleak deliberation. *'Agere contra'* – to act against the feelings, to consider the 'other' always in the perspective of some rational end, is proposed as the safest rule. How is the role of reasoned will and calculated choice to be understood in the anatomy of love?

The life of Christ was certainly marked by the stress of spiritual conflicts (as in Gethsemane). But the gospel does not present a picture of cool calculation. Christ's was a given life, attention squandered on the seeker and the needy, time gobbled up by the crowds. Yet the man for others does not appear as one without feeling or without need. He wept over the unreceptive Jerusalem: 'How often have I longed to gather your children as a hen gathers her brood under her wings'.[16] We hear unmistakably, the plangent echo of tenderness. He wept at the grave of Lazarus and felt compassion for the hungry crowds in the desert. One of the disciples was referred to matter-of-factly by his fellows as 'the one Jesus loved'.

Love requires choice. Jesus chose to continue on the road to Calvary. Love sometimes leads to a choice which flies in the face of self-interest and personal affection; which acts counter to the pressures of fear and sadness, even to those of self-doubt. Yet love does not stand entirely within the logic of rational motive and conscious decision. What really moves us in this life is the flow of our deep feelings, the luminous and life-giving images which lie below the patina of thought. *Eros* provides the energy and the vision for our lives. *Logos* gives our decisions shape, direction and order. It is our deep feelings that drive us to decisive action, both to heroism and to tragic failure. Ideas and propositions, moral concepts and principles, in themselves, can only point, advise, reveal implications and predict consequences.

We love many things – natural things and artefacts. We love more than one person. We may love ideas which give order to experience and ideals which give it worth; as some people are said to have a love for truth or a passion for justice. Christians love the God they have not seen but in whose gracious presence they live. They love Jesus, in whose shadow they continually stand. There must be an order in our loves, as there is a hierarchy in our values. We do not shoot to kill, even though we disapprove of lawlessness. I may love Mozart passionately. But if a sick-call comes, I have no right to hear out the last movement of the Clarinet Concerto before going to the hospital; nor would I wish to do so.

Nor would I wish... motives which impel to actions distant from our present interests, motives based on principle and duty, can also be irradiated by love. It is the business of moral education and of spirituality also to make this happen. When Richard Lovelace wrote

> I could not love thee dear so much
> Loved I not honour more[17]

he was expressing such an ordering of loves. We need not particularly approve of his 'higher alternative':

> True a new mistress now I chase
> The first foe in the field;
> And with a stronger faith embrace
> A sword, a horse, a shield.[18]

But it is clear that the feelings he expresses about courtly valour ('mistress', 'faith', 'embrace') are not in the order of passionless reason. War and patriotism represent a higher passion. It has been so with many.

When St Augustine wrote, 'love and do what you will', he was certainly not proposing a recipe for moral anarchy. He is envisaging a state where 'what you will' has passed from being transient whim or even rational choice to become a passion of the heart. It has been said of prayer that, persevered in, we discover through it what we really want. Our deep needs are uncovered. We recognise that what we really want is not this or that thing from which we started. It is peace of mind or it is integrity or it is perfection. It is the love of God and his grace.

Levinas has written that the first perception of the other – strange, disconcerting, with its own being not to be assimilated, its own rights not to be gainsaid – establishes within us the awareness of morality and is the groundwork of love. Necessarily, conflicts arise as love expands, and these are not always because love is fragile and threatened. It may be because we genuinely love things and people which are incompatible. The girl I love is passionately in love with someone else. What shall I do? Go in and try to win her, for such is my need and such (I may think) her real interest? Or take another and more painful path? What I do is unlikely to be a clinical decision of the mind. 'The heart has its reasons' is sometimes used as a superficial slogan. But it is from the intelligent heart that solutions to such conflicts most fruitfully come.

The dilemmas of love are not always, not often, conflicts between reason and passion. Rationality is involved. I try to foresee the consequences of the alternatives which are offered and to fit them into a moral pattern in which I believe. But moral decision is also a drama of feeling. Those feelings which sustain my commitment to the moral order are also awakened, and love is in these, whether of another, of a country, of justice or of God. These are the feelings which lie at the roots of life, where the springs of action are coiled. These feelings do not grow in a day, nor without pain, this reality which Wordsworth calls his 'moral being':

> Dust as we are, the immortal spirit grows
> Like harmony in music; there is a dark
> Inscrutable workmanship that reconciles
> Discordant elements, makes them cling together
> In one society. How strange that all
> The terrors, pains and early miseries,
> Regrets, vexations, lassitudes interfused
> Within my mind should e'er have borne a part
> And that a needful point, in making up
> The calm existence that is mine when I
> Am worthy of myself.[19]

It is said that Sigmund Freud, when asked to express his view of the meaning and purpose of life in a small capsule, replied: *'lieben und arbeiten'*, to love and to work. His words have a pulling power but an over-simple allure. Liam Hudson[20] remarks that because Freud was a psychologist and most of those who use his words also follow that profession, the emphasis is thrown forward on to *lieben,* on to the field of life where love presides. Psychologists are especially interested in human relations, in their smooth and fruitful organisation. Of course, tax inspectors and professional cricketers are also concerned with human relationships, but since they do not make a profession of these, they are less likely to transform them into a norm. It is the temptation of psychologists to assume that human relations are of such paramount importance that everyone should be like psychologists (or as they would wish themselves to be).

Hudson, however, remarks that to some, the world of work seems of greater importance, and these are not necessarily to be counted among human failures. On the contrary, they include some of the greatest creative geniuses. Beethoven, for instance, was one whose personal life was in ruins even as his masterpieces were being composed. Such individuals, to our enormous benefit, are able to channel their vital energy into the creative field in which they are so gifted.

The distinction itself, love versus work, seems of limited value. Few things in this world are purely relational. Most relationships involve tasks, jobs, mortgages, projects and common interests. On the other hand, work is almost always directly or indirectly set in a context of relationships, with managers and colleagues, with family and friends, with God and one's conscience. Rarely is it to be found isolated in a cool, dry, germ-free place.

Apart from matters of context and perspective, is there not a deeper kinship between love and work? To perceive otherness, in one way strange and alien, is to enter also into the world of good and evil. To be aware of the other is to be aware of rights and duties. But it is not a closed, constraining perception. It opens the way to the possibility of relationship. It leads us to see not so much what *is,* as inescapable limit, rather what *can be* as creative possibility. The foundation of morality, the germ of love, the source of imagination, it discloses to us the exhilaration of beauty, the light of meaning and the strength of truth.

This radical connection between love and work is most evident in the calling of artists and scholars, those whose achievements we often refer to as 'labours of love'. The making of art as a work of love is difficult and always threatened. Often, what lies at the roots of bad art is emotional self-indulgence. A bad artist is under the illusion that the immediate and urgent expression of his feelings is of interest to humankind. He may not lack technique, but fails in that distancing, that recollection of emotion in tranquillity, that careful making of an artefact which is a true form for feeling. As often as not, what bad art lacks is humility and patience. In the Russian Church, icon-painters are required to undertake quite an arduous spiritual formation before they are allowed to paint. This is not to improve the quality of their brushstrokes. It is to ensure that their art is not restricted to the assimilative mode of personal expression, but concentrates rather on making the image which embodies the 'other' and reaches towards the infinite.

The peril of scholarship is that it may envisage its work solely in the perspective of mastery; grasping, seizing, assimilating experience into a system. This is, among other things, a temptation of power. For the vigorous mind to have grasped something is to have demolished its otherness. What is needed also is to look at experience so as to learn its meaning before fitting it into categories. Huxley wrote of the true scientist that he is one who 'sits down before the facts like a child'. There is a place for receptivity and contemplation as well as for curiosity and conquest. Socrates saw this when he taught that the roots of the good and the true are intertwined. Scholars need moral and spiritual qualities beyond a ruthless devotion to truth in the limited terms of concepts and logic. This is especially true of theologians. Like the Russian icon-painters, they stand in need of a spiritual discipline, not to sharpen their wits but to ripen sensibility and nourish vision. Coleridge wrote: 'Deep thinking is only attainable by a man of deep feeling. All truth is a species of revelation.'[21] Serious study has its moral and emotional prerequisites. 'True learning begins in wonder, goes on in humility and ends in gratitude.'

Does love also touch the grind of the worker on the assembly line? Externally, it may well do. He does his work for the love of others, perhaps for the love of God. Auden's phrase, 'the routine courage of the worker', suggests that there may be more to it than that; because the dawning perception of love is also the first glimmer of duty. We are able to put love even into routine tasks because we see, perhaps confusedly, that behind the acceptance of the daily chore is the acknowledgement of duty, respect for the other and a faint glint of the infinite.

For those called to ministry within the Christian tradition, the connection between love and work should be especially close. 'Feed my lambs … tend my sheep'; the metaphor of Jesus carries the force of attentive care, even tenderness. Pastoral work, however, can often be arduous and unrewarding. This may be because of the task itself. If your job is church administration or keeping the books, it takes a courageous and visionary faith to leap the gulf between these humdrum activities and the upbuilding of the Kingdom of God. It may be because of the frustration which Isaiah expressed:

> They will hear and hear again and not understand;
> see and see again and not perceive.[22]

This frustration can engender a sense of helplessness, of inability (perhaps for personal, perhaps for cultural reasons) to make God's truth bright and effective in people's lives.

Other aspects of pastoral work – teaching and preaching for instance – which touch the mind and the heart, can be shot through with creative joy. As the artist makes something which lives beyond and after him, as the scholar uncovers something which has its own indwelling truth, so the pastor may enable a mind to live in its own freedom and truth, may turn a heart from bondage into the fresh fields of love and hope. Here, where ministry flourishes, the distortion of love also becomes apparent. A teacher wants her students to think as she does. A preacher is tempted to play on the superficial emotions and so produce instant (and often transient) results. Among the satisfactions of ministry, the demands of love may be forgotten; to recognise and respect otherness, to resist the sly temptations of assimilation and dominance.

Martin Büber's phrase, 'confirm the other', eloquently and positively expresses these demands. 'Affirming' is often said to be the first stance required of a counsellor or a spiritual director. Of course, to affirm does not mean to approve of the attitudes and behaviour of the one thus strengthened. It may well be that the counsellor hopes that both of these will be profoundly changed. The force of affirming is: remain other. It is 'be yourself, the self which is already a good self, unconditionally loved by God and by me'. But, it implicitly adds: learn to know your true self also, to see its real potential, its limitations, its likely or actual distortions.

Love in all its forms begins in the awareness of the other as a separate centre of being and life. Out of the 'buzzing, booming confusion' of the early days, significant patterns begin to emerge in experience: significant patterns, for interpretation comes before perception. We do not first perceive chaotic masses of sense-data and then arrange it in a meaningful way. To perceive is not just to see, hear, touch and taste; nor is it even the sum of all these. To perceive is to make sense of this data, first in relation to our own interests, then (what a quantum jump) in its own being.

This awareness has folded up in itself the notion of rights and the corresponding notion of duties. Those who never achieve it, we call psychopaths. It forms the groundwork of the moral sense. In it we discover the germ of that natural love which St Paul says God has 'written in our hearts'; that law which begins, 'Thou shalt not kill', and ends, 'Thou shalt love thy neighbour as thyself'.

Yet awareness of the other, though the most crucial expansion of our consciousness, is also threatening. The other is resistant, is indigestible. It is not to be drawn into the lungs like air, sucked into the mouth like milk or shaken like rattles. This conflict between respecting the independent life of the other and the desire to assimilate it, remains permanently alive in us, although usually in increasingly sophisticated forms. The course of true love rarely runs smoothly. It is necessary to formulate moral principles and laws in order to prevent the distortion of love. These laws may contain the conflict between recognising and assimilating, but they often hurt. Being human and fallible formulations, they sometimes cripple true love, as well as protecting it from its own inherent flaws. Love, the source of expansion, vitality and joy, is sometimes the cause of deep pain.

> Who then devised the torment? Love.
> Love is the unfamiliar name
> Behind the hands that wore
> The intolerable shirt of flame.[23]

The living flame of love, according to St John of the Cross, is one which burns as well as warms and enlightens.

Love exists first between the 'I' and the 'other' and generates its own imperatives. It lives also within the human community; and in this context, commitments and interests may clash, and the need for order and principles is recognised. Society and culture formulate this order into laws and conventions. Through these, the general good, the interests of minorities and the rights of the individual are (it is hoped) protected. Finally, for the Christian, love also exists within the perspective of God's covenant. Its ordering is directed by God's word uttered in Scripture and tradition; so that love may form God's undistorted image in human persons.

Love lives then within a series of widening structures and these may be numerous and complex. In a society where 'This country's planted thick with laws from coast to coast', in a culture or a religion where behaviour is rigidly and comprehensively codified, may not these structures become a dead hand; transforming love into a system of correct behaviour, quenching its native (and essential) spontaneity?

They may, of course. It is possible to weave so dense a mesh of laws, rules, conventions, protocols, manners, decorums and respectabilities that love, trapped inside it, cannot get its breath and dies. For love begins when I recognise and accept the other. Should it totally lose that spontaneous freshness in the coils of a system, it is lost: just as faith begins in the astonished recognition of God in Christ and draws its vitality from keeping that recognition alive. If it is totally dispersed into a moral (or spiritual) system, its true nature is lost. It becomes a fanaticism or blind conformity. It loses gentleness and human warmth.

The novels of George Eliot illustrate how, in the unbearably stuffy conventionality of the Victorian age, only the toughest forms of creativity found their way to the surface. Women especially were so enmeshed, not only in manners and conventions, but also in presuppositions about their nature and role in the world, that the lot of those with creative talent was almost hopeless. There are (or have been) systems of moral theology which tried to legislate for every conceivable human action in every conceivable set of circumstances. These result in so huge and so heavy a code of behaviour that the heart is crushed, its reasons in ruins. Those who escape, as though hacking their way out of Hampton Court maze, may somehow thrive *(All for Love or The World Well Lost)*, but they often suffer crippling isolation.

But structures vary. We do not speak of conventions, rules, laws and principles in the same tone or with the same seriousness. In the perspective of love, we rightly dismiss respectability and having nice manners as trivial. But going a little beyond them we come to courtesy. We sense that we are approaching some kind of dividing line. For courtesy is close to kindness. We are among the virtues and virtues hold love in very different hands from the rough and ready grasp of conventions or rules. Virtues are habits but they are habits which safeguard our deep choices. So the bloodline of true virtues goes back to love's origins.

Rules suggest either playing a game or belonging to a club. If you want to play the game properly, you need to observe the rules. If you belong to a club you ought to keep them. There is a degree of loyalty here, but not one we take with any great moral seriousness. Laws we do take seriously.

Behind laws lies the authority of Church or of state. That of the state we may accept perforce. That of the Church we acknowledge through a personal commitment. In either case (despite frequent dilemmas) a moral obligation is acknowledged and a real connection with the sources of morality established. The structures which seem to constrain love are not all external, the results of living in communities. Within ourselves too are principles and values which direct and sometimes restrain our actions.

Love has to live and find itself within a variety of structures. We chafe against these and sometimes find them stifling. But we also sense them to be necessary; to be sometimes part of the order of things. *Eros* needs *logos* for control; 'If you cut down every law in the land', says Thomas More to his son-in-law Roper (fresh from Germany and Luther), 'and you're just the man to do it – will you be able to stand upright in the gale that will blow then?' Love is a powerful force in life, in which our energy finds its source, in which God reveals Himself. It also contains inner flaws like geological faults, waiting to crack. It retains the drive to assimilate the other. You love a girl with tenderness and respect but also feel the urge to eat and digest her. Or there is a conflict between love. You love Lucasta but you love honour too. What is to be done? Hierarchies, principles, laws and virtues arise out of this dilemma. If these are formulated and imposed sensitively and sanely, they do not destroy love but rather channel and liberate it to be its true self. When love is seen at the heart of Christian faith, the law itself becomes invested with God's love, a way to him, an expression of his will. Hence the surprising and touching love of the law of God, found especially in the Psalms.

> I have sought you with all my heart,
> let me not stray from your commands
>
> I treasure your promise in my heart
> lest I sin against you.
> Blessed are you, O Lord,
> teach me your commands.[24]

Chapter 5

AT CHARTRES
A Meditation on the
Simple and the Complex

If you leave Paris towards the south-west, you must pass under the runways of Charles de Gaulle Airport; hearing the rumble of the jets as they taxi towards take-off; towards Beijing and Wellington, towards Port-au-Prince and Antananarivo. It is a moment which focuses modern life, its mobility, its plasticity, its intimidating technological leaps. As you go on it is possible to avoid the Autoroute l'Océan, avoid the sense of being emptied out and squeezed into another system. Further north a lesser road proceeds more gently through Rambouillet and Maintenon. Leave that and you find yourself on the ample and fruitful plain of the Beauce. The River Eure is crossed by hump-backed bridges which link the villages. At some point, depending on the clarity of the day, two spires appear on the horizon. They are paired but not matched; the one tall and slender, the other rather stubby and highly wrought. The traveller, though a 'pilgrim of the absolute', will not find at the end a classical masterpiece of symmetry and order. As it looms closer it becomes plainer that this is an empirical building, shaped by history and occasion, by devotion and ambition, by daily concerns, mystical vision and the effluxion of time. Continue towards it and any little road will funnel you into the broad square that faces the cathedral church of Our Lady at Chartres.

To go into this church is to enter a world of light which is quite different from the light in which we conduct our daily affairs. It is a 'dim religious light', no doubt, but not with a gloom that blurs and confuses. On the contrary, it is sharply luminous, a full though quiet radiance which seems to dye the air so that it is almost breathed. So we lift our eyes to the windows which, in the morning or the evening sun, in high summer or at the winter solstice, filter the light to us in dense patterns of meaning, of event and circumstance, of folly and heroism, of pain, of love, of glory. It is the opposite of Shelley's image:

> Life like a dome of many-coloured glass
> Stains the white radiance of eternity.

It is the exact opposite of that. The glass of Chartres transforms the colourless and abstract daylight, bodies it out into the meaning of human choices and happenings, into the history of salvation; into a world which seems at first glance to be complex and bewildering.

'All human life...'

We are led first (by the guidebook, but rightly so) to the middle of the nave to contemplate the cathedral's oldest windows. The first to catch the eye depicts the tree of Jesse. A tree trunk springs from Jesse's heart. It spirals upwards, branch, tendril, leaf, through David, Solomon and the Kings of Judah to the Virgin Mary and to Christ. It is the genealogy of Jesus. It is a graceful spiral. We follow it upwards and see that it closely resembles a huge fleur-de-lis, symbol of royal France. We observe that the ancestors it passes through are a line of royal kings. To the artists who painted this picture, political loyalties were not irrelevant to faith. On the contrary, they were prominent in its weave which, in the age of Christendom, comprehended everything that was of concern to the individual or important in society.

Further into the nave affairs of a humbler sort are commemorated. The fishmonger presides over the baskets of his wares in the shop and pushes his barrow through the streets looking for customers. Above him, tier upon tier, the story of his patron saints is told. St Anthony gives his belongings to the poor. In the desert he wrestles with Satan, is victorious, finds peace in his cell. More spectacularly, St Paul the hermit is fed, during a thin season, by a crow. When he dies lions come out of the desert to bury him. On the other side, the drapers and furriers pursue their trade, measuring, fitting, trimming, adjusting. Above them the sad history of St Eustace unfolds. He is converted by the words of Christ spoken through a stag at bay before his weapons. But his life takes many sad turns. He is thrown into the sea by a surly shipmaster. He loses his two sons to wild beasts. He is finally, but triumphantly, martyred.

In the window of the Zodiac the peasant's year is traced. He keeps warm by the fire in the dead of winter. In March he prunes the vines, in April tends the wheat. In May he hunts, in June gathers in the harvest, in August threshes the corn. September is the grape harvest, October is for wine-making. In November the pig is killed. The window records the passing of time, portrays the recurring rhythms of human life. The order of nature, from seed-time to harvest, from midwinter to the summer solstice, gives glory to God.

The windows present a vast panorama of an age and of a faith. Here, writ large, are the great truths of faith: the redemptive work of Christ in his birth, death and resurrection; the coming of the Spirit; the life and glory of Mary and the saints. Woven in with them are numerous small dramas, some legendary and dramatic, others simple and familiar, the everyday doings of butchers and carpenters. It may seem at first (so dazzling is the visual impact) that these events and figures are put together anyhow, without plan or pattern, exuberant and rich but random. Yet shortly, themes assert themselves, the series of covenants between God and man, the theme of routine courage and heroic sacrifice. The order here is created by the great windows of Christ, crucified and in glory; of the descent of the Spirit; of Our Lady *'de la belle verrière'* presiding, 'most gracious advocate' over the wedding at Cana and over our human loves, inadequacies and partings. It is not an order of military precision or of logical exactness. It is an order of the imagination.

Friedrich Nietzsche is improbably said to have remarked, 'The Protestant reformation was the revolt of the simple against the complex'. He was right. The Reformers wished quite properly to renew the Church. They suspected that its corruption was closely connected with its complexities; the power vested in its hierarchical order; its doctrinal system subtly organised and firmly imposed; its rich but perhaps idolatrous devotional life focused on Mary, on the exuberant variety of saints. The Reformers looked to sweep all this away to recover a *'sancta simplicitas'*. But where to discover this holy simplicity? Where but in the Scriptures taken (naturally) in a literal sense and directed to each believer in an unmediated way. Time would show that this was not a straightforward road to follow. An uneasy sense would grow that the Scriptures must in some way depend on the Church. Otherwise how had they come about? The Enlightenment, the impact of reason and science would throw a new and disturbing light on the question; what do the Scriptures actually mean? Nevertheless, it is easy to see how the cry 'Scripture alone' must have seemed to offer a way of undermining the vain and elaborate structures of ecclesiastical complexity, a return to the primitive and the simple.

The suspicions of the Reformers were in one way right. There was a connection between the complexity of Catholic tradition and the corruption they saw in Church life all around them. In another way they were wrong. The connection was not the one that they supposed. Why and how does faith become complex?

This has indeed been the underlying theme of this book and we have seen some of the answers.

From mystery to proposition

The most striking answer (not necessarily the most important one) is found in the development of doctrine. This, we have seen, grew out of practical concerns; and out of the decision (not perhaps carefully thought-out but providential none the less) to take the plunge into the world of human reason, to despoil the Greeks of their concepts, to speak the first words in that difficult, risky, age-old, unending conversation between faith and reason. The first practical concern which triggered this momentous step was the natural desire to understand and so to feel easy in one's mind. Secondly, there was the need to express Christian faith in a way that was clear and comprehensive as well as forceful. The gospel was for all. It should not continue to be imprisoned by the discipline of the secret within small groups of initiates like the ancient mystery religions. It should hold up its head and carry its own conviction in the broad pastures of the Graeco-Roman world. There arose the need to defend it against the charge of being confused and contradictory or subversive of the social order, or of culture or of humanity itself. Finally the conflicts which arose within the Christian community ('Is Jesus truly God?') could not always be resolved by greater devotion or by prayer, or even by the decrees of Church authority. They needed to be laid out in the clear air of reason, where logical criteria might apply, where positions could be clarified and compared, where the way to a resolution might eventually appear.

It was easy for this process to develop its own energy and take on its own life. In time it grew into a massive and impressive logical system, subtle, sophisticated, generating fascination among its practitioners, becoming a field within which those responsible for Church order could control the thinking of the community. It is easy to see how, for some, it began to seem that this doctrinal system was the hard reality of the faith. Even those who did not fall into this 'category mistake', have often been impelled to press on with this language of faith in ever more subtle ways. Those who retained a keen sense of the mystery of faith were aware of the higher slopes of that mystery stretching ahead, always beyond their reach. To climb a mountain is to come upon a whole series of illusory summits. When we arrive at them, further vistas open up, larger worlds to be conquered, higher peaks to be climbed.

These summits are illusory only as summits. They also represent substantial achievements. We can stop and rest and admire the view and rightly think that some worthwhile progress has been made. Doctrinal achievements too are not tentative or provisional. Because the mystery still stretches ahead of us, this does not mean that we could scrap everything that has been done and start off again by a fresh route. Doctrinal achievements are substantial and indeed irreversible. They are enshrined in the Creed, in the tradition of the Church. They are, some of them, canonised by the indefectible teaching authority. There is an absoluteness about the great doctrinal statements. Yet it is not uncommon to absolutise them in a different and mistaken way. This is to imagine that divine truths and the mystery of faith can be dissolved into doctrinal propositions without remainder; the dynamic but elusive reality of faith transformed into the sharp but lifeless clarity of propositions. It is as though a climber reached a small summit and believed that now there was nothing beyond him, only the empty air and the sickening drop into nothingness. The pilgrimage of faith is not like that. It does not end up in this sublunary world in a final self-satisfied arrival, not even in Rome or Lourdes or Jerusalem. The pilgrim of the absolute is always in John Donne's position:

On a huge hill
Cragged and steep truth stands and he that will
Find her, about must and about must go.

It is an image which contains not only the oblique and roundabout character of the journey towards truth; but also the sense of a journey never completed, of the spiritual courage required and the discipline of humility.

From symbol to ritual

What is sauce for the goose is sauce, *mutatis mutandis,* for the gander. Christian faith over time, developed a complexity in its liturgy as well as in its doctrine. Those who thought about liturgy and planned it, rightly perceived the great power of symbol and rite, of times and seasons, of fasts and feasts, which are the ingredients of the liturgical language of faith. They saw that it was an idiom which proclaimed the mystery of faith perhaps more effectively than any other. So it is easy to see how liturgy too might develop its own life, its principles, its distinctive ways of working, develop into a self-contained 'realm of meaning'. Indeed it is necessary to go some way along that road; to see how the liturgy works, what its methods are, its rhythms, the forces that play in it, if it is to be able to speak. But it is only a short step from that to the moment in which the liturgy becomes rigid, top-heavy and unbalanced, and in doing so, pulls up its roots. What results is ritualism, an outlook according to which the rites are carried out for their own sake, for the impressiveness, the order, even the beauty inherent in them. Ritualism is, at its worst, formal and sterile, at its best, a kind of religious aestheticism. The acid test which reveals it is the rigorous enforcement of rubrics and the quenching of inventiveness and spontaneity. No doubt it was such rigid and apparently empty formalism which led the Reformers to reject the liturgy of the Church and look for a style of worship which both spoke to the heart and breathed the air of an earlier and simpler world. They came upon a liturgy which had lost its bearings. The bread it should have broken for the world in both word and sacrament had gone stale. It had lost its power to nourish.

From response to rule

Our first moral impulse as believers is to respond to God. It is how we say Yes to God in our hearts and in the conduct of our lives. This proves to be not so easy as it sounds. It is straightforward enough (though not easy) to love God in our hearts and to mean well. But beyond that there are many choices open to us in our personal lives and in the forum of public life too. St Paul's sharp words to his early communities underline this point. There are some ways of behaving which cannot be harmonised with the gospel. There are some which contradict it shockingly. There is a moral order in the world. How is it to be discovered and made plain enough for us to see what the pattern of our lives should be?

We have already seen how the notion of natural law helped to answer this question. This moral order is somehow written in our very nature. It is written there by God himself. All of us have a conscience. We are able to perceive (though maybe in a shadowy way) how we ought to act and what choices go against the grain of our being. We must not kill the innocent. Sexuality is not for trivial and casual use. If we act against these perceptions the grain of our being resists. It becomes ragged and unkempt. We become uneasy and out of sorts with ourselves. The laws of nature need to be spotted and need to be formulated; so also do the laws of the gospel which form the basis of that tradition of moral wisdom which we find in the life and practice as well as the formal teaching of the Church. In *A Man for All Seasons* Robert Bolt puts these words into the mouth of Thomas More:

> 'This country's planted thick with laws from coast to coast
> … and if you pull them down – and you're just the man to
> do it, who would be able to stand upright in the winds that
> would blow then?'

His interlocutor, Roper, counters:

'It's as I thought. The law's your god.'
'Roper, you're a fool,' More answers, 'God's my god'.

This small dialogue concentrates a number of points. A world stripped of laws would indeed be a savage climate. Only a figure of heroic proportions could survive in it. St Augustine's 'love and do what you will' is advice to be taken literally only by saints. Yet there is a point also in Roper's riposte. More was a man of sufficiently large vision to see the reality behind the laws. But the vision of others may be short-circuited. *Facilis decensus Averni.* It is easy to descend into legalism. And at the end of the tunnel of legalism lies the large fact of idolatry. Laws map the moral world for us. They make it navigable. Yet they sometimes take on a life of their own, grow and grow until they occupy the whole of our moral and spiritual space.

Sometimes then, doctrine becomes doctrinaire, liturgy slips into ritualism, the morality of love and grace is distorted into legalism. This process may become clearer in the light of the psychological phenomenon of dissociation. Dissociation occurs when a system within the personality takes on a life of its own, becomes self-sufficient and exists independently of, or even counter to the good of the whole. Examples would be a phobia, like the fear of open spaces, or an anxiety neurosis. Systems like these are resistant to common sense, even to self-interest. They do not yield to a good talking-to. The advice to 'pull yourself together' is precisely what their victims are unable to act upon. On the contrary they frequently suffer from severe inner conflict.

We learn the languages of faith so that we may understand it more clearly, celebrate it more aptly, live it more confidently. But sometimes these languages develop their own head of steam and get loose in the weave of faith, a source of unease and disturbance rather than of strength and peace. They may find their own *raison d'être* rather than serve the whole fabric of faith. St Paul writes, 'If the body were all eye how could it hear? If the body were all ear how could it smell?' What is true of gifts and talents is true also of the languages of faith. They find their authentic accent only in being part of the greater whole; and only in this way do they remain rooted in that luminous and life-giving experience of faith which is their one source of freshness and energy. If they pull up these roots we are well and truly and painfully impaled on the horns of von Hugel's dilemma. One source of complexity in faith is simply the immensity of God and the finitude of human minds and hearts. That immensity is refracted in the optic of time, of circumstance, of concept and symbol, of principle and law. We see not a simple white light but a spectrum. The spectrum itself is fascinating and beautiful. We may absolutise it, give it an ultimacy which it does not possess. It may revenge itself, drag away from its roots, beach us on an illusion of finality, stuck half-way to where we ought to be.

Knowing the bluebell

The complexity glimpsed in the light and shade of Chartres cathedral, however, is of a different kind, both more profound and more elusive. It is not to do with logical analysis or finely-tuned systems. It is to do with the fact that faith both comprehends and is expressed by the daily doings of saints and sinners, of fishmongers and furriers, as well as apostles and martyrs. It is expressed by the doings of the Lord and what was done to him as much as by the grand sweep of theological systems. It is immersed irrevocably in the concrete and the particular, in the 'stained, skeined variety' of human affairs.

It is often said today, and rightly, that in its life and mission the Church should attend carefully to the question of enculturation. There is almost always a close, if shifting, unsteady relationship between faith and culture. For culture is the way people live their lives and order their relationships; it is the attitudes and values which hold society together; it is the whole way of life of a group of people. Occasionally it has seemed that a culture was so hostile to Christian faith that flight was the only answer – either literal flight into the desert, or the construction of an enclosed and self-sufficient life which provides protection at the price of isolation. But most often the Christian community forms a more positive relation with a culture – if not a happy marriage, at least a decent working relationship. Faith in this case, which is marked by a culture on the one hand, alters – even forms – the culture on the other. The battle cry 'enculturation!' warns faith, and warns the Church also, not to become a prisoner of a culture; not to become so marked by a culture as to become inaccessible to people whose ways of thinking and acting are very different.

All this is true. Yet it rests on something deeper. Behind the difficult issue of faith and culture lies the question: What is the nature of faith in the world? What is its very being in relation to daily affairs and historical cataclysms, in relation to those 'joys and hopes, fears and anxieties of the men of our time'. The windows at Chartres attest vividly that faith is inextricably tangled with these things. Catholicism is a religion of the felt and the handled, of the remembered and the cherished, of seasons of grace and sadness, of holy places and family traditions, of the sensed and the symbolic, of the everyday and the eccentric, of the grittiness of life and its multifoliate variety, of the historic, of the present, of the incarnate.

Gerard Manley Hopkins looked attentively at a bluebell ('what you look hard at seems to look hard at you') and said, 'I know the beauty of Our Lord by it'.[1] His words could be read as simply the fancy of an aesthete, a pious thought to decorate a serious argument. Yet behind the thought lay a much deeper issue. For one thing this 'inscape', this disclosure of an inner meaning, was by no means restricted to the conventionally beautiful in the Romantic manner. He perceived it throughout nature. Crystals in mud and the cut of hailstones equally cried out 'what I do is me, for this I came'; so also did the wasting figure of the dying Felix Randal, his 'mould of man, big-boned and hardy-handsome'.

Hopkins' problem was that in traditional Catholic philosophy, individuation occurs through matter. So, to love the individual bluebell, or indeed the individual person, is to become immersed in matter, to open wide the gate of the senses; also implicitly to close the gate of mind and will which, properly purified and humbled, is the only reliable way to the world of spirit and truth. The idea that individual sense-experience might offer clues or jolts towards deeper truth was of course familiar to Hopkins as it is to any reader of poetry. These lines of Browning illustrate it well:

> Just when we're settled there's a sunset touch,
> A fancy from a flowerbell, someone's death,
> A chorus-ending from Euripides,
> And that's enough for fifty hopes and fears
> The grand Perhaps....

Browning, well buttoned-up in a kind of Romantic agnosticism, could only be jolted as far as the 'grand Perhaps'. Maybe these experiences presage, even embody the presence of some deeper, transcendent meaning in the world. Hopkins wanted to go much further: 'I know the beauty of Our Lord by it.' He wanted to say that in our experience of nature and of life, it is not only the large generalisations about its contingency, about its patchy order, which reveal the deep structure of reality. Also its quirkiness, its tough, persistent individuality, its bewildering variety, its fugitive beauty reveal, if in fits and starts, the real presence of grace.

Luckily for him Hopkins came upon something which enabled him to see that what he had here was more than an aesthetic fancy. He came upon Duns Scotus and his idea of *'haeccitas'*, 'thisness'. It was the idea that the individuality encountered in the hurly-burly of experience reflects God's presence as truly as do the large abstracts which are filtered out of it. Scotus' best known and most contentious teaching was that the Incarnation of God would have happened even without the fall. God's being made flesh and dwelling among us was not an emergency plan put together when things went amiss. It was in the nature of reality. In Christ 'everything in heaven and on earth was created … and all things are held together in him' (Col 1:16-15). God is mirrored everywhere in the world, in its particularities as much as in its large general patterns. And so:

> Glory to God for dappled things
> For skies of couple-colour as the brinded cow[2]

Perhaps Hopkins, enthusiastically taking up Scotus, got hold of the wrong end of the stick and misinterpreted him. Often we pick up insights and distort them to meet our urgent concerns. Still, what Hopkins made of Scotus is an important idea in itself; one especially relevant when we are thinking about the languages of faith and about its complexities.

The particular

For many centuries, almost from its beginning, Christian faith has been confronted by the *scandal of particularity;* since Porphyry asked why Jesus was not a wise philosopher like Socrates, who thought universally and died nobly. The scandal is that Christian faith is focused on one short life which was lived in one historical epoch, through one culture, one language and which was patchily documented. Surely, the scandal runs, if God were to reveal himself to human beings it would not be done in this eccentric way. Surely if a message is called the Word of God it should be a cosmic philosophy revealing truths about the universe of great depth and vast scope. A life that ended in apparent failure, a teaching cast largely in parables and paradoxes, can hardly qualify for the title.

Here is G. K. Chesterton having a characteristically spirited stab at this question. 'If Moses had said God was an Infinite Energy, I should be certain he had seen nothing extraordinary. As he said He was a Burning Bush, I think it very likely that he did see something extraordinary. For whatever be the divine secret and whether or not it has (as all people have believed) sometimes broken bounds and surged into our world, at least it lies on the side furthest away from pedants and their definitions, and nearest to the silver souls of quiet people to the beauty of bushes and the love of one's native place.'[3] Hidden perhaps a little in this lively polemic is the truth that a human person is the most authentic image of God. God is not mirrored by 'humanity' or by any other large abstraction. Only a single human being can bring the 'thisness' which makes us exclaim, 'I know the beauty'; can add that luminous perception to the broad sweep of thought which comprehends supreme spirit and self-existence and infinity. The individual life – a *person* comes – in its sayings and its doings, is marked by contingency and incompleteness as well as other things. This may lead us into some difficult and puzzling territory. It may lead us to say that God has in *some* sense suffered, in *some* sense failed; in *some* way shares in, makes common cause with our human brokenness. Well, Amen. Let these partial truths stand.

Languages and realities

Language is sometimes presented as though words and sentences were counters which stand for realities in the mind, as a mating move stands for a strong position on the chessboard. They are, it is sometimes implied, a set of marks on a page or vibrations in the ether which could be changed for a different set, and lo! another equally adequate language appears. It is an impoverished and mechanistic view. Language is not a set of inert counters but a dynamic force in our minds and in our lives. Through language we explore our experience and uncover its meaning. It leads to insight and insight leads to control. We are able to learn from experience and so choices open up, so freedom and responsibility begin. Through language 'the biological individual becomes the rational and historic person.'[4]

To speak of 'languages of faith' is to use a metaphor. Yet metaphors are not fantasies. The languages of faith resemble English or German in substantial ways. They uncover the meaning of the experience of faith. In doing so they can strengthen faith and extend its range in our lives. They do not exactly have a grammar and syntax. But they have distinctive ways of working which we can get the feel of, become fluent in. To say this is not to imply that a mature faith must be highly literate; that a mature Christian must be able to manage the concepts and logic of theological argument, to participate reflectively in the liturgy, to wrestle with complex moral dilemmas. No, not that. What we should look for, what we should try to promote in Christian education, is that these several languages of faith should have *some* foothold in all our lives, even a slight one. Without that minimum sense of complementarity of many-sidedness, faith is unlikely to grow in a balanced way. Distortions are almost certain to occur.

These distortions in their extreme form come to resemble a dissociation in psychology. Doctrinal exactness, ritual correctness and moral legalism sometimes take an obsessional turn. They become loose cannons firing, as in a mighty battle, on friend and foe indiscriminately. This can occur even with the first and most basic of the languages, that of story. Stories – 'foundational myths' – lie close to the roots of the experience of faith itself. Yet without stiffening they may grow into purely subjective myths; a world of personal fantasy which lends a certain romantic aura to life, but loses contact with those realities which faith professes in its doctrines, celebrates in its liturgy and affirms in its moral life.

To use the metaphor of 'dissociation' is perhaps to over-dramatise the case. It is not common that the whole weave of faith is ruptured by a distorted enthusiasm for one of its languages; though we do sometimes come across instances where an obsessive concern about doctrinal correctness or with legalistic morality brings about the downfall of a diocese or a parish or an individual life. Commoner and closer to us is the experience of getting lost in a language of faith; getting so tangled in its thickets that the larger vision becomes occluded; that the experience of faith seems small and distant, as though viewed through the wrong end of a telescope. Take, for example, the formulation of the doctrine of the real presence of Christ in the Eucharist. Sometimes this discussion becomes so dense with metaphysical subtleties that we feel stranded in a dark wood of concepts; the light failing and the straight road lost. Take, more topically, the expression of the doctrine of original sin. Here the lucid simplicities of faith-experience seem ambushed in the deep shadows of anthropology and prehistory. Again the issues of justice and peace stand today in the foreground of the mind of Christians. Yet to formulate our faith response to these issues is often to face perplexing problems. Considerations derived from economics, politics and commerce seem immediate and compelling, seem perhaps to mask and mute the imperatives of the gospel. Or perhaps we are facing a personal moral dilemma and the arguments which surround it (say natural law arguments) do not seem at all to chime in the register of the gospel. They strike a flat, dead, philosophical note. The vivid experience of faith and the tangled thickets of its formulation easily come apart. How is Humpty-Dumpty to be put and held together?

'Pure faith' and evangelisation

Faith is often contrasted with belief, with theology, with religion, with doctrine, with attitudes, with values, with this, that and the other until we wonder what can be left. Is there anything more substantial than the smile of the Cheshire cat? Is there a 'faith' which precedes all knowledge and formulation, which is pre-conceptual and pre-logical, which can be filtered out and kept in a cool, dry, germ-free place? No there is not. Even in its very beginnings faith acknowledges that something is the case. It professes a loyalty to someone: 'Master, to whom shall we go?' It espouses, however vaguely, a better way of life, *'la vita nuova'*. In a sense of awe and reverence it contains the germ of worship. Already the beginning of faith embodies something, however rudimentary, of its languages. It has already gone a few paces down those roads. What is it then, to return to von Hugel's dilemma, that makes the experience of faith so compelling, whereas the idiom of its languages is often so lacklustre? It is surely that in the first case, the components of faith are held together in a different focus. They are not ordered in the extended line of logic and understanding. They are fused in the narrower, more potent lens of discipleship, of commitment, of love, of deep, personal meaning. In a similar way, preaching refocuses the contents of tradition through the purpose of conversion of heart. Prayer also draws on the languages of faith but fuses them into a personal relationship.

Evangelisation is an urgent concern for all Christians, especially today when we find ourselves in new and bewildering circumstances for which there are few precedents. It is a temptation – a seductive hope – to suppose that evangelisation might be able to leave aside worrying cultural circumstances, doctrinal and moral complexities; that it might be able to speak in a disembodied way to arouse 'pure faith', *'cor ad cor loquitur'*. But this is a chimera. Better think of it in another way. Now, as always, evangelisation involves the languages of faith. It is not the disembodied voice of 'pure experience'. Yet these languages – the content of tradition – are to be restructured, redirected, reassembled, so as to reflect our own keen experience and to speak to that of others. *'Cor ad cor loquitur'* – Newman's motto, 'heart speaks to heart', is indeed a key phrase. But the heart has its reasons, it has its own understanding; it learns to speak, in its unique way, a variety of languages.

We have seen already that, among the languages of faith, some lie closer to experience, some more distant from it. Story is the first language and it remains the most potent for 'sharing faith'. In the early days, the apostles preached the story of the Lord's life, and it was this which communicated their faith – 'Brothers, what must we do?' Yet, although the language of Scripture has remained central, we have seen even in the New Testament how their preaching spoke with effect chiefly to those whose minds were formed by Jewish tradition and by the Old Testament.

Even in the earliest days, St Paul was looking for a different idiom in which to address the Graeco-Roman world. In our times – even more secular, more distant from the cultural origins of Christianity – to share one's personal story of faith seems the most effective, and the most honest, means of evangelisation. It is a story told in a context of friendship, of solidarity with the 'joys and hopes, the fears and anxieties' of our fellows. In this way it both reflects the reality of our faith and is open to the experience of others. If, in the telling, our story exposes our vulnerability and brokenness as well as tracking the paths of God's grace in our lives, so much the better. Personal stories, however, need to be enriched. To learn to speak the languages of faith causes the narrative of our lives to enter that many-sided vision of Christian faith which reflects the mystery at its heart. The larger story of Scripture and history, the sharp clarity of doctrine, the profound meanings of symbol and sacrament, the discourse of love and nature and holiness weave this web. One of the functions of the various languages of faith is to correct each other.

Education in faith

Between evangelisation and education there is not set an impassible gulf like that which separated Dives and Lazarus. The educator, like the evangeliser, is dealing with the languages of faith. Education seeks to extend understanding, to promote sensitivity and reflectiveness, to develop faith in a fourfold vision rather than a single optic. In doing this, it risks moving further and further away from the vivid reality of experience into the atmosphere of the theology lecture or the religious education lesson – sometimes dull, sometimes academically remote. In what spirit, through what approaches might an education in the languages of faith retain 'the roll, the rise, the carol, the creation' of experience? How can it follow Aquinas' principle, 'the true object of faith is not formulations but realities'? It is a question which takes, like a bold toreador, von Hugel's dilemma directly by the horns.

A clue which sets us off along the right road can be found in these oft-quoted words: 'true learning begins in wonder, goes on in humility, and ends in gratitude.' It is a saying which both spans the gap between concept and feeling ('wonder', 'gratitude'), and also the gulf between intellectual enquiry and moral and spiritual quest ('humility'). Sitting down humbly before the prospective truth is a discipline – a tough discipline – which transforms detached investigation into personal and spiritual pilgrimage. This was Newman's way also, when he argued the vanity of approaching 'truth without homage'. 'Let your opinions be the result', he wrote, 'not of mere chance reasoning or fancy, but of an improved heart.' This approach proposes that the languages of faith can be learnt only in accordance with their nature; that the ethos and character of the mysteries of faith is quite different from the truths of logic and empirical science. It is easy to misunderstand this. You might think it meant that a heavy dose of piety could sufficiently sweeten what is intellectually slipshod so that people would swallow it. You might think that 'reverence' meant a prejudice favourable to some conclusions and hostile to others, so distorting evidence.

Of course in some cases that might be so. There is a false

humility which can be an excuse for not thinking, for not facing difficulties honestly. That this need not be so can be seen in Milton's tough and elegant defence of freedom of the press. 'Where there is much desire to learn, there of necessity will be much talking, much arguing, many opinions; for opinion in *good* men is but knowledge in the making.'[5] Milton is in favour of the cut and thrust of public debate; of facing the rigour of this and refusing to sweep difficulties under the carpet. He is also emphatic that only in good men does hotly contested opinion become knowledge. It is not that truth belongs to the morally perfect, not that the saints have all the best tunes. Rather it is the case that in the search for truth the virtues of humility and of honesty as well as hard work are not extras. They constitute a moral and spiritual dimension without which the pilgrimage towards truth slips easily into being a set of random voids, a collection of superficial enquiries. It is the maintenance of this dimension which keeps the languages of faith alive and vivid.

Living in the word
> If you make my word your home
> You will indeed be my disciples;
> you will know the truth
> and the truth will make you free! (Jn 8:31-2)

In a memorable and disturbing image, the Letter to the Hebrews pictures the word of God as a double-edged sword. It pierces 'between joints and marrow, between soul and spirit'. It 'sifts the purposes and thoughts of the heart' (4:12). We feel the bite and jar of a bone-saw as it probes and penetrates; shudder as the tense frontiers of our being are invaded. The sifting, the laying-open of purposes and thoughts is even more disconcerting. We cherish our privacy. It is ringed with defences and illusions and we begin to feel these crumble. We are disturbed, perhaps deeply troubled by this for 'humankind cannot bear very much reality'. The word of God is a challenging word. It is not stayed by excuses nor diverted by a fog of confused motives. It does not connive with weakness or evasion. Although it is recognised as a surgeon's knife which 'questions the distempered part', its cutting power retains a certain terror.

But that is not all that can be said. There are other images. The word of God is like a seed which is sown in a field. Some of it falls on good ground, some among thorns, some where the soil is thin, some on the footpath. The fate of the seed depends on where it lands. Some grows well, some badly, some not at all. In this image, the word does not have threatening sharp edges. On the contrary, its power is inside the husk. It is dense with vitality, with the beginnings of new life. It comes to us, not to cut away at our tissue but to lie there until we do something about it. It can be rejected or swamped by other concerns. It can be accepted, lazily or whole-heartedly. It is a gift laid helpless and vulnerable on the earth. If it is accepted, then the painful process of probing and cutting will begin; but the green blade will rise as well.

Different again is the image with which this section began. The word of God is not like a surgeon's knife, nor like a seed which lands to root itself or not as the case may be. 'If you make my word your home'; the word of God is a house into which we are invited. The invitation is not to make polite conversation at a cocktail party nor to spend a relaxing weekend before catching the early train on Monday. It is to take up permanent residence as a member of the family. It is to come as a disciple, as a learner, therefore, a listener who will pick up the family lore and catch the family spirit. It is an invitation also to be fully at home, to join in meals and share the chatter in the kitchen; to dig the garden in spring and be enveloped in the peace of winter evenings.

What is it like, the house of God's word? It is large and rambling. Its architecture and amenities are of uneven quality. Perhaps it has a Tudor front, a Regency wing on the right, and to the left a Victorian horror. At the back, slightly decayed are the old stables. Here someone has added a bathroom. Someone else has thrown out a conservatory from the dining-room. Inside it is gracious, spacious and welcoming, if a little hotch-potch. It needs to be when you think of the huge variety in the personalities and habits of its occupants. It has been home to mystics and geniuses as well as warlords and heroes. It has housed many saints and not a few blackguards; as well as countless quiet people of whose silver souls Chesterton wrote. It has been the arena of heroic sacrifice, of fierce quarrels, of quiet holiness, of much achievement, much failure, much thought and much love.

When you live in a house for a long time it seems to absorb something of the dramas, the joy and sadness of your life. It was in this room that A and B fell in love; it was from the hall there that they went out to be married. Here X died and we carried her out towards that other great house. On this very spot took place that momentous conversation which so drastically changed the direction of my life. Memory can be a nostalgic escape. But memory is also a powerful force which is, von Hugel wrote, 'a strong and interior, a lasting yet voluntary bond of union between our successive states of mind, and between what is abiding in ourselves and what is permanent within our fellowmen'. Memory holds us together and it spills over into a grace of place. The house is permeated by it and binds us to itself. Of course we do not love the house indiscriminately. There are rooms where we do not go often, some which we may deliberately avoid. We are not meant to be passionately attached to the roof tiles or devoted to the central heating system.

The house of God's word is also spacious and rambling. It has its large classical façades and its small curious outgrowths. Although it is a house of God's word, that word is made flesh. The house is marked by humanity and history, it 'wears man's smudge and shares man's smell'. It is permeated by the chequered, stumbling, triumphant history of the Body of Christ. A household, long-established, develops a loyalty – perhaps subdued and critical, but tough – to itself, to its tradition, to its values. The house of faith, too, puts down tenacious roots into the very substance of being. Yet the buildings which rise from these foundations bear the mark of our time-conditioned lives, of the diversity of our understanding and feeling, sometimes even of our fashions and fancies. We are not obliged to love the whole house indiscriminately. It may be draughty in some seasons. It may seem ill-adapted to modern living. As we have seen, there is a hierarchy of truths. Some stand simple and plain in the centre of things. Others are complex elaborations which serve their purpose but do not stand in the heart of the house. We are called to be at home there and so to love the whole house; but not with a flat, level kind of love. We are not obliged to linger in the lumber-room or clamber about in the attic.

'Make my word your home.' The Lord's call is an invitation to truth and freedom. The freedom is in being a child of the house and knowing ourselves as members of God's family, safe from the crippling enslavement of anomie and lostness. The truth is in the ability to approach the ultimate mystery through the languages of faith. It is a way of knowing which is oblique and partial. It is not knowledge which we are meant to do up in neat packages and present cockily to others as a set of ultimate facts. We are meant, rather, in humility, to draw others into this way of understanding, to throw open to them the door of the great sprawling house of God's word. It is a house in which we have space to live and breathe, to relate to others, now intimately, now stormily. It is a house in which we are never bored though sometimes afflicted; often also surprised by joy.

NOTES

Introduction
1. Quoted in T. S. Eliot's 'Journey of the Magi', from a sermon by Lancelot Andrewes.
2. Matthew 5:3.
3. John 8:58.
4. John 11:25.
5. John 14:5.
6. F. von Hugel, *The Mystical Element in Religion*, J. M. Dent, 1961, p. 1.

Chapter 1: The Truth of Imagination
1. C. Dickens, *Hard Times*, Oxford University Press, 1989, p. 5.
2. D. H. Lawrence, 'Why the Word Matters' in *Phoenix*, Heinemann, 1936, p. 535.
3. Plato, *The Republic*.
4. P. Sidney, *The Defense of Poesy*.
5. T. W. Tilley, *Story Theology*, Michael Glazier, 1991.
6. Matthew 11:16-18.
7. John Keats, Letter to Benjamin Bailey, 1817.
8. Coleridge, *Biographia Literaria*, Everyman, p. 140.

Chapter 2: 'A Blessed Rage for Order'
1. Wallace Stevens, *Selected Poems*, Faber & Faber, 1953, p. 99.
2. Arius, *Thalia* (The Banquet).
3. Gregory of Neocaesarea: quoted in Fuller (ed.), *The Christian Idea of Education*, Harvard University Press, 1975, p. 159.
4. J. H. Newman, *The Development of Christian Doctrine*, London, 1898, p. 40.

5. Newman, ibid., p. 36.
6. Vatican II, *Dogmatic Constitution on the Church.*
7. J. H. Newman, *The Grammar of Assent,* Longmans Green, 1889, p. 95.
8. Newman, ibid., p. 92.
9. Newman, ibid., p. 88.
10. Newman, ibid., p. 83.
11. Newman, ibid., p. 95.
12. Romans 5:12, 18.
13. Ephesians 1:10.
14. J. H. Newman, *The Tamworth Reading Room.*
15. B. J. Lonergan, *Method in Theology,* University of Toronto Press, 1990, p. 52.
16. W. Walsh, *The Use of Imagination,* Chatto & Windus, 1960, p. 65.

Chapter 3: Feeling and Form
1. J. H. Newman, *Grammar of Assent,* Longmans Green, 1889, p. 99.
2. W. Walsh, *The Use of Imagination,* Chatto & Windus, 1960, p. 229.
3. P. Levi, *The English Bible from Wycliffe to Barnes,* Constable.
4. J. Locke, *Human Understanding,* Routledge, p. 321.
5. R. S. Thomas, *Collected Poems,* Bloodaxe Books.
6. D. H. Lawrence, 'Why the Novel Matters' in *Phoenix,* Heinemann, 1936, p. 536.
7. Edwin Muir, *Autobiography,* Graywolf Press, 1990.
8. B. J. Lonergan, *Method in Theology,* University of Toronto Press, 1990.

Chapter 4: The Truth in Love
1. Aquinas, *Summa Theologiae,* 1-2, Q91 art 2.
2. Vatican II, *The Church in the Modern World,* 16.
3. G. Chaucer, Prologue to *The Canterbury Tales.*

4. Shakespeare, *Hamlet.*
5. K. Rahner, *Situation Ethics in an Ecumenical Perspective.*
6. 1 John 4:16.
7. Dante, *Paradiso,* Canto XXXIII.
8. *Love Alone: the Way of Revelation,* Sheed & Ward, 1989.
9. E. Levinas, *Ethics and Infinity,* trs. Richard Cohen, Duquesne University Press, 1985.
10. Levinas, op. cit.
11. Levinas, op. cit.
12. Levinas, op. cit.
13. Balthasar, op. cit.
14. Balthasar, op. cit.
15. Luke 14:25.
16. Matthew 23:37.
17. *To Lucasta: on going to the wars.*
18. Op. cit.
19. W. Wordsworth, 'The Prelude', l. 340ff.
20. L. Hudson, *Contrary Imaginations,* Penguin.
21. Coleridge, *Letters to Poole,* 1801.
22. Isaiah 6:9.
23. T. S. Eliot, 'Little Gidding', *The Collected Works of T. S. Eliot,* Faber & Faber.
24. Psalm 118:10-12.

Chapter 5: At Chartres
1. G. M. Hopkins, *Notebooks.*
2. G. M. Hopkins, 'Pied Beauty'.
3. Quoted in *G. K. Chesterton,* Maisie Ward.
4. W. Walsh, *The Use of Literacy,* Chatto & Windus, 1960, p. 229.
5. *Areopagitica.*

SELECT BIBLIOGRAPHY

The reader will see that this book draws heavily on the works of J. H. Newman and S. T. Coleridge. Among Newman's works I have used especially:

The Grammar of Assent, Longman Green, 1889

The Essay on the Development of Christian Doctrine, Montague Pickering, 189?

The Idea of A University, Dent, 1915

University Sermons, Oxford University Press.

For Coleridge see *Biographia Literaria,* Everyman, Dent and *The Portable Coleridge,* a useful and accessible collection of extracts.

See also the two outstanding essays by William Walsh in *The Use of Imagination,* Chatto & Windus, 1960.

Chapter 1:

John Shea, *Stories of God,* Thomas More Press, 1978; *Stories of Faith,* Thomas More Press, 1980.

John Navone, *Towards a Theology of Story,* St Pauls, 1974.

T. W. Tilley, *Story Theology,* Michael Glazier, 1991.

J. D. Crossan, *The Dark Interval,* Polebridge, 1988.

See also the series by various authors which includes *How to Read the Old Testament; How to read the New Testament* (both 1981); *How to Understand the Sacraments,* 1991; *How to Read Church History,* 1989, all published by SCM Press.

From a different perspective, there are some highly illuminating chapters in David Tracy, *A Blessed Rage for Order,* University of Chicago Press, 1995, and *the Analogical Imagination,* Crossroad Publishing Company, 1985.

See also: *Selected Poems and Letters* of John Keats (Ed. Gittings) Heinemann; E. M. Forster, *Aspects of the Novel,* Edward Arnold; *Phoenix* (ed. MacDonald), Heinemann, contains a great deal of D. H. Lawrence's spirited criticism as well as the articles I have quoted.

Chapter 2:

M. Schoof, *Breakthrough,* Gill & Macmillan, 1970, a useful account of recent Catholic theology in a historical, developmental perspective.

A. Dulles, *Models of Church,* Gill & Macmillan, 1987, and *Models of Revelation,* Orbis Books, 1992 which give an insight into the structures, patterns and conflicts in theological thought.

See also:

Monica Hellwig, *What are the Theologians Saying Now?* HarperCollins, 1993.

Fuller (ed.) *The Christian Idea of Education* (especially the articles by John Courtney Murray and Georges Florowski), Shoe String Press, 1975.

N. Lash, *Change in Focus,* Sheed & Ward, 1973.

A. Nolan, *Jesus Before Christianity,* Darton Longman & Todd, 1978.

J. L. Segundo, *The Community Called Church,* Gill & Macmillan, 1973.

Chapter 3:

This chapter draws substantially on the work of Suzanne Langer, especially: *Feeling and Form,* Routledge & Kegan Paul, and *Philosophical Sketches,* Oxford University Press.

See also:

T. Klauser, *A Short History of the Western Liturgy,* Oxford University Press, 1979.

M. Dujarier, *A History of the Catechumenate,* Sadlier, 1982.

T. Guzie, *The Book of Sacramental Basics,* Paulist Press, 1982.

L. Boff, *St Francis,* SCM Press.

SCM Series, *How to Understand the Sacraments.*

C. G. Jung, *Modern Man in Search of a Soul,* Routledge & Kegan Paul, 1984.

A. Moreno, *Jung, Gods & Modern Man.*

Chapter 4:

The ideas and texts from von Balthasar come from *Love Alove: The Way of Revelation,* Sheed & Ward, 1989.

See also:

K. Kelly, *New Directions in Moral Theology: the challenge of being human,* Geoffrey Chapman, 1992.

B. Hoose, *Received Wisdom, Reviewing the Role of Tradition in Christian Ethics,* 1995.

E. McDonagh, *Gift and Call,* Gill & Macmillan.

C. S. Lewis, *The Four Loves,* HarperCollins, 1960.

L. Hudson, *Contrary Imaginations,* Penguin.

Chapter 5:

G. M. Hopkins, *Poems* and *Notebooks.*

See also: Robert Bernard Martin's admirable biography, *Gerard Manley Hopkins: A Very Private Life,* HarperCollins, 1991.